# Untamed Nature

This book belongs to _____

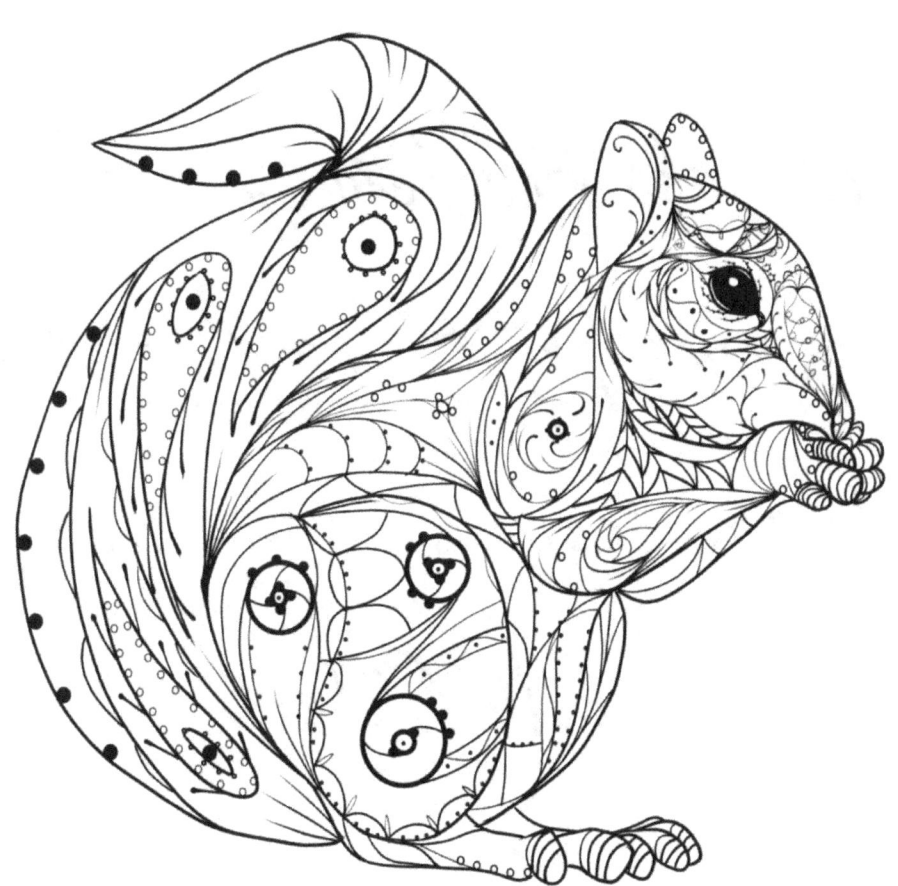

*Those who find beauty in all of nature will find themselves at one with the secrets of life itself.*

*~ L. W. Gilbert*

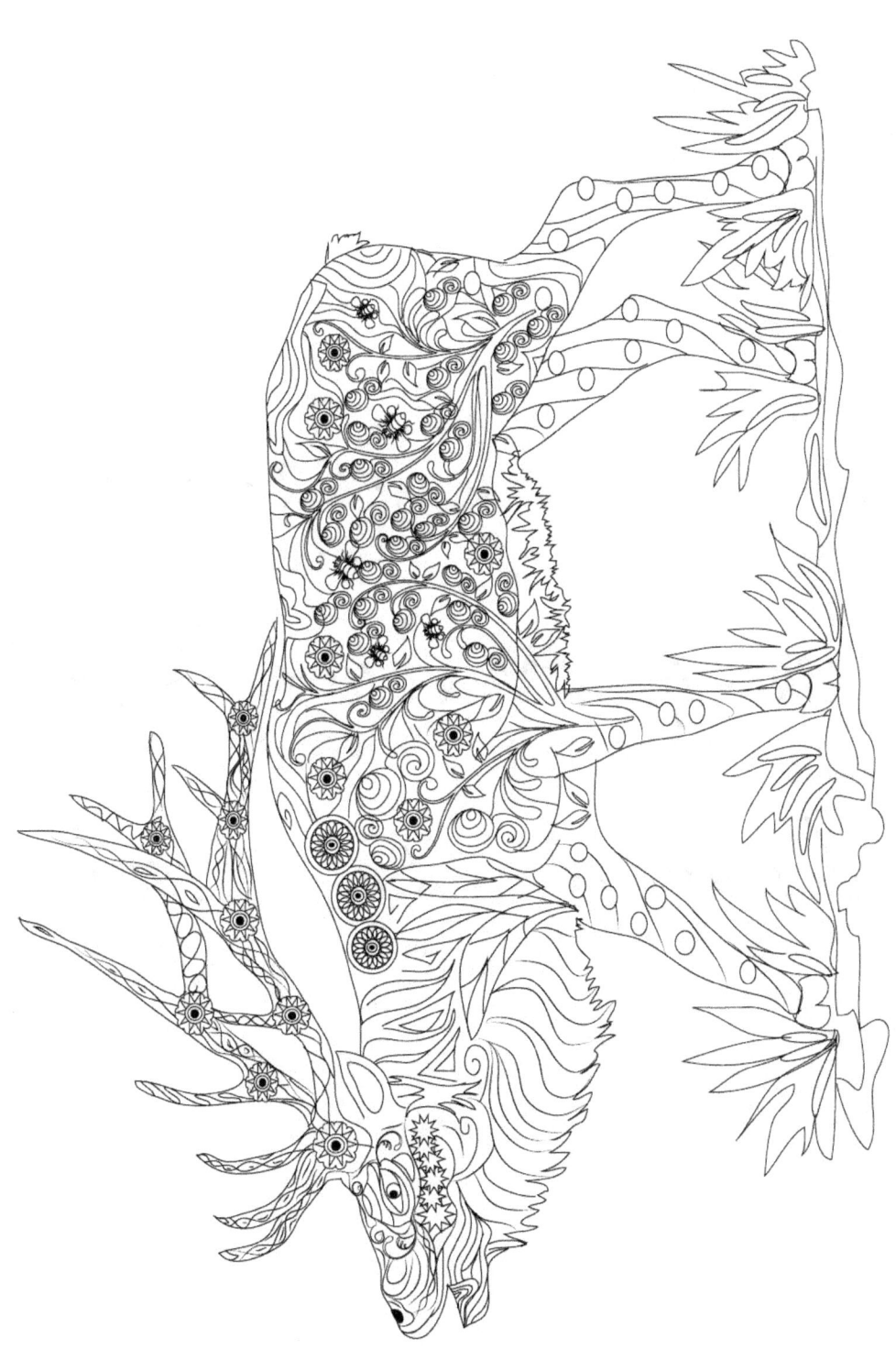

Your mind will answer most questions if you learn to relax and wait for the answer.

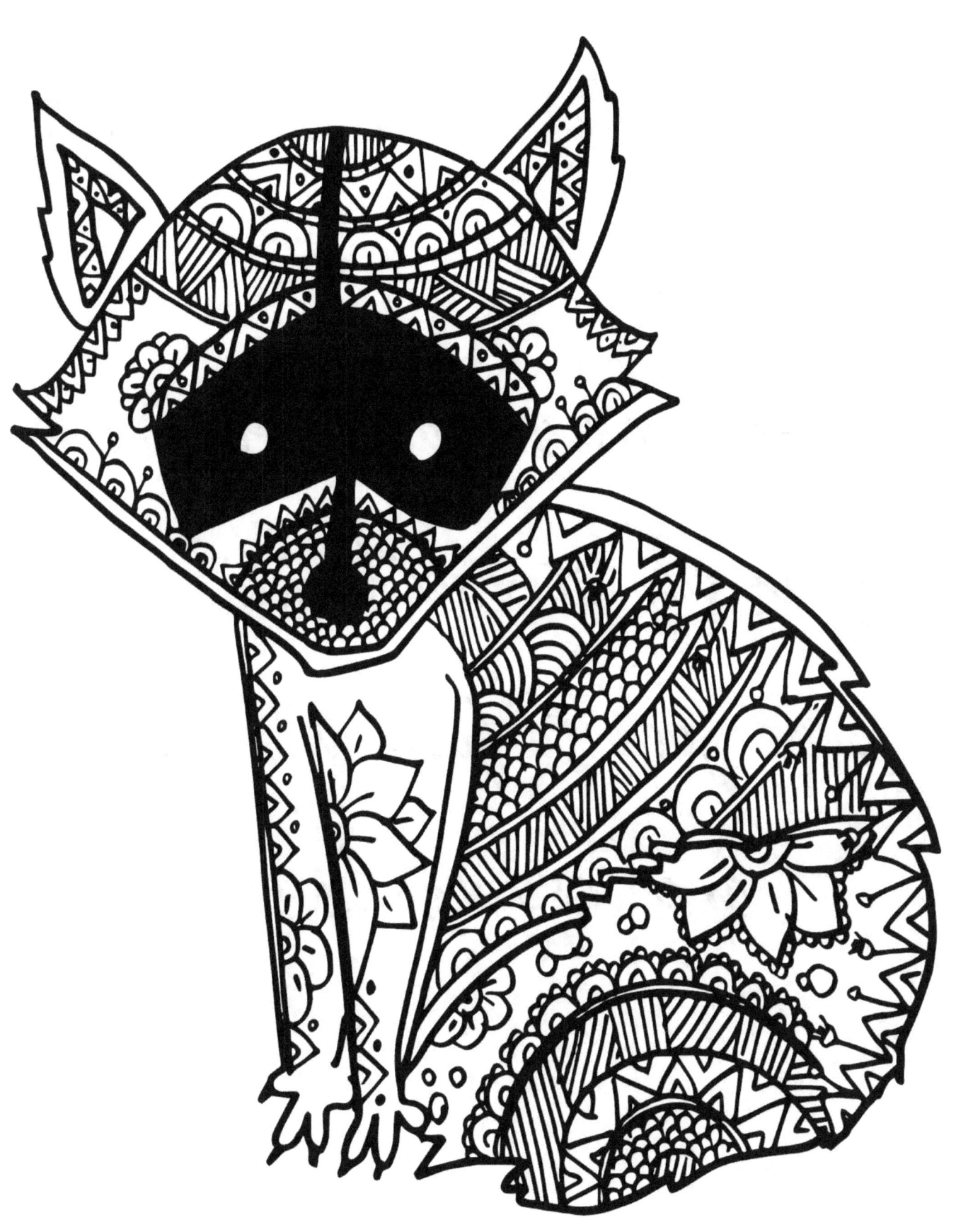

Sometimes you don't realize your own strength until you come face to face with your greatest weakness.

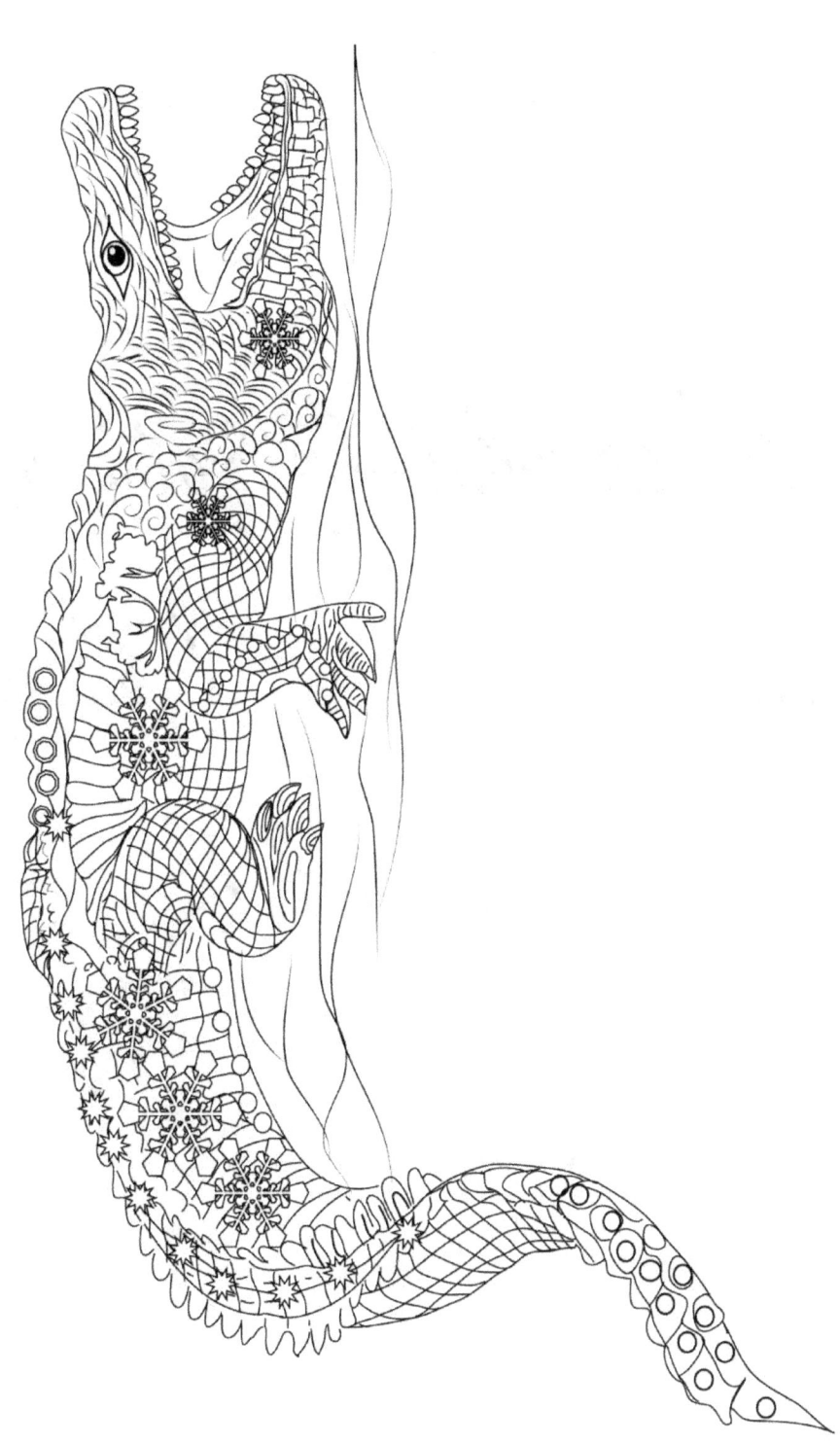

I did absolutely nothing and it was everything I thought it would be.

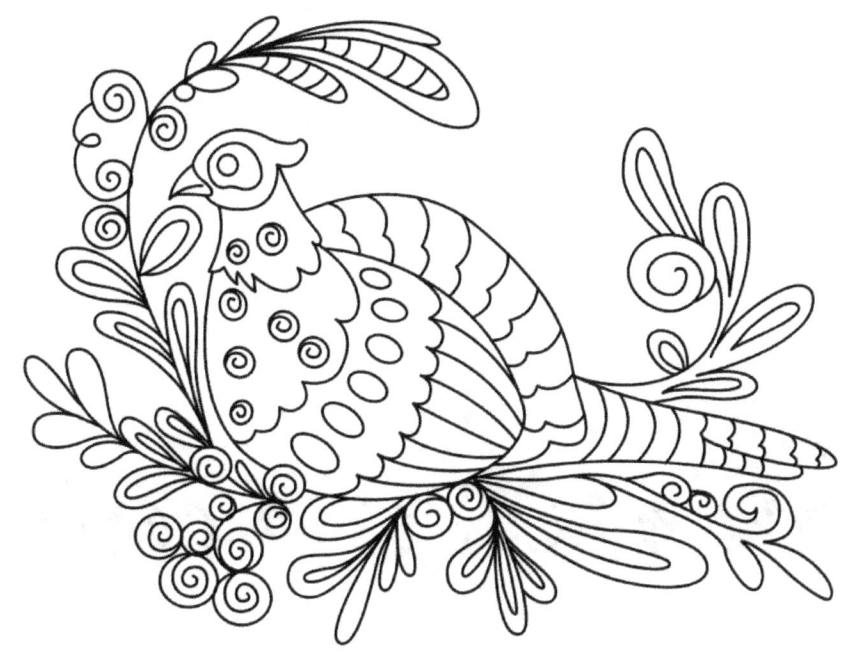

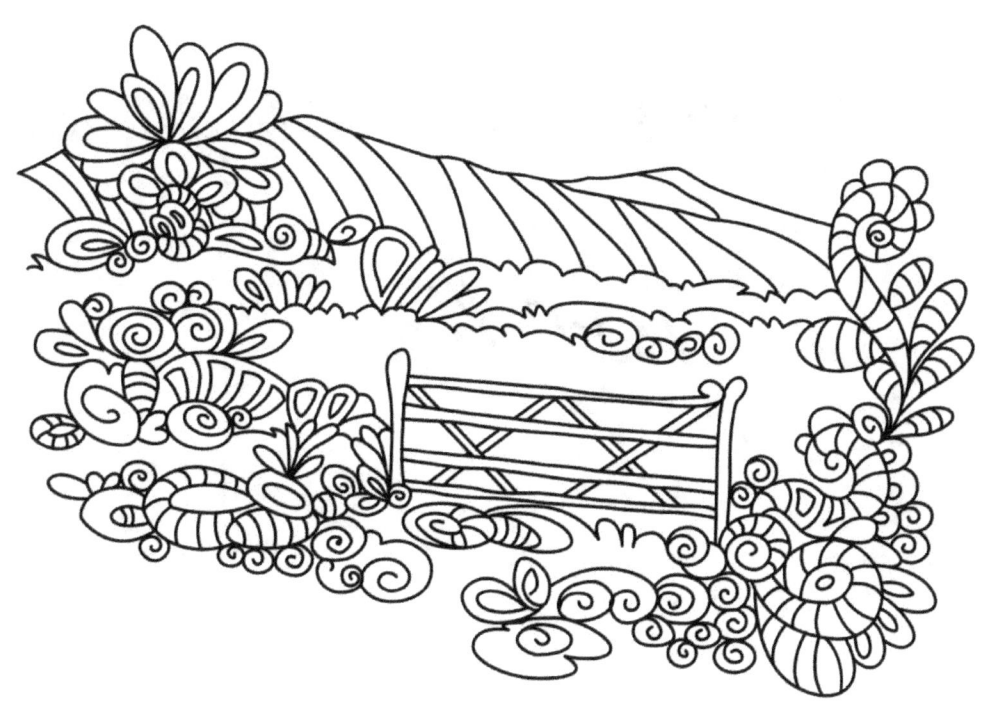

When you try to control everything, you enjoy nothing. Relax, breathe, let go and just live.

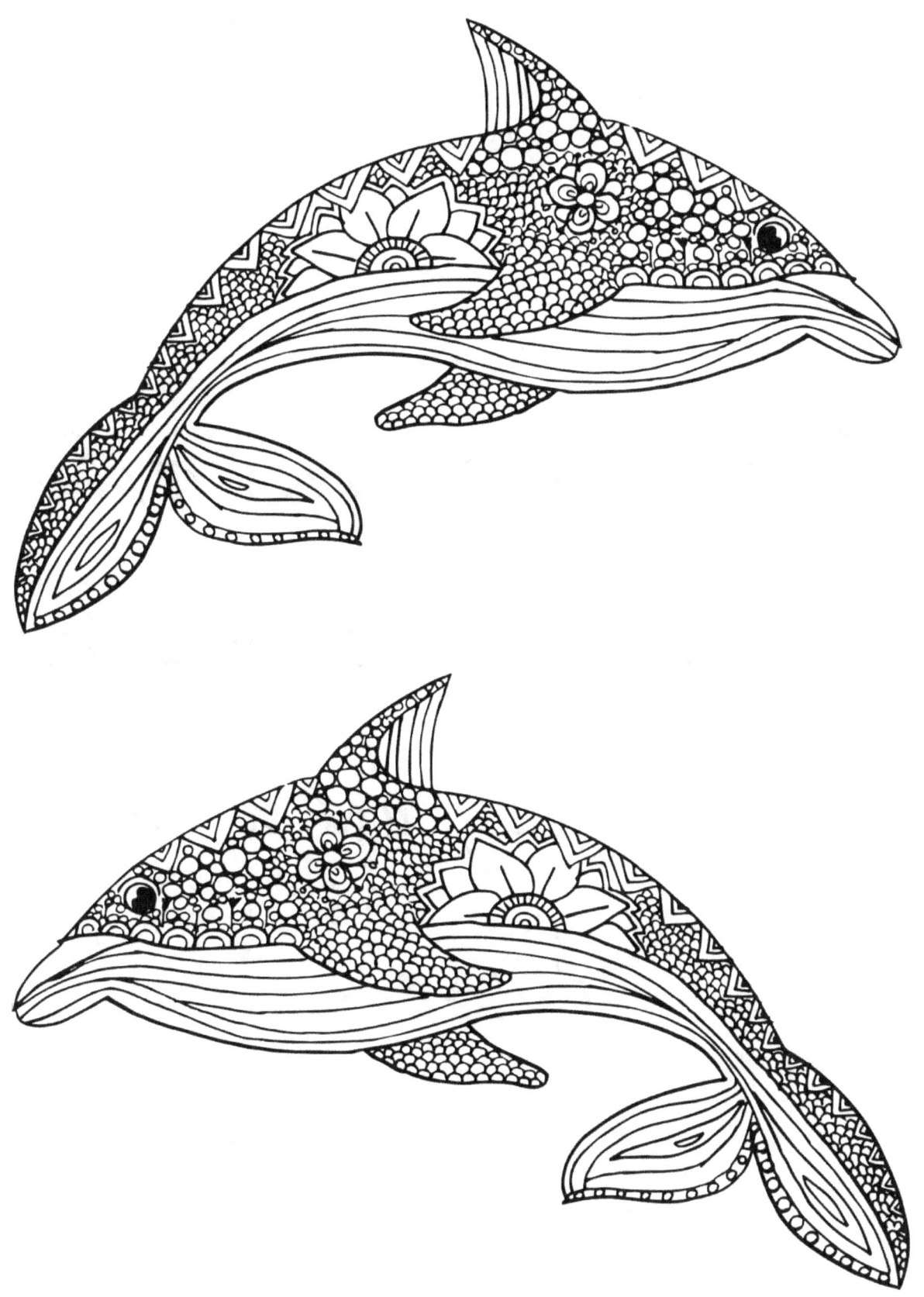

You don't always need a plan sometimes you just need to breathe, trust, and see what happens.

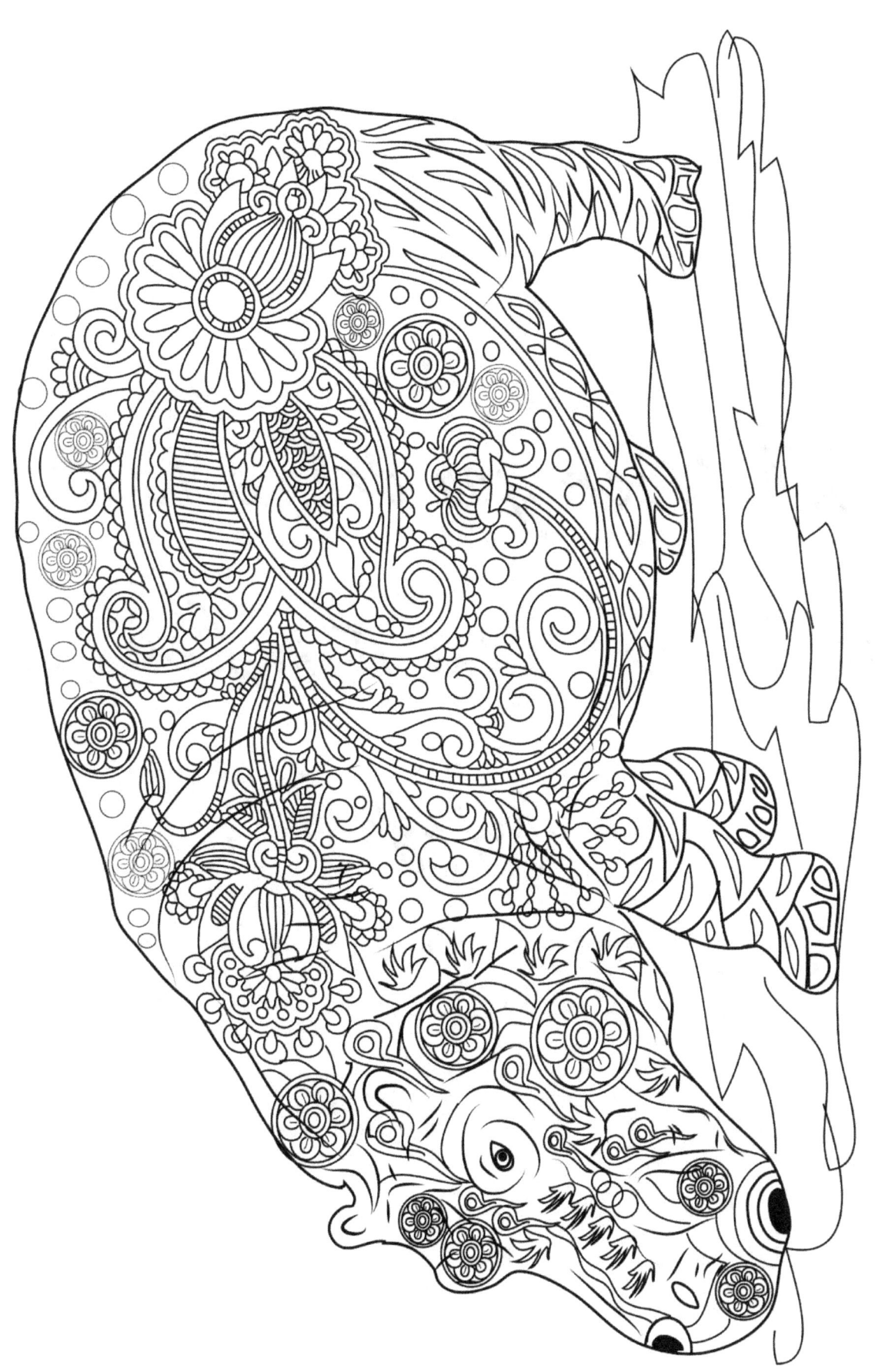

Whatever you decide to do, make sure that it makes you happy.

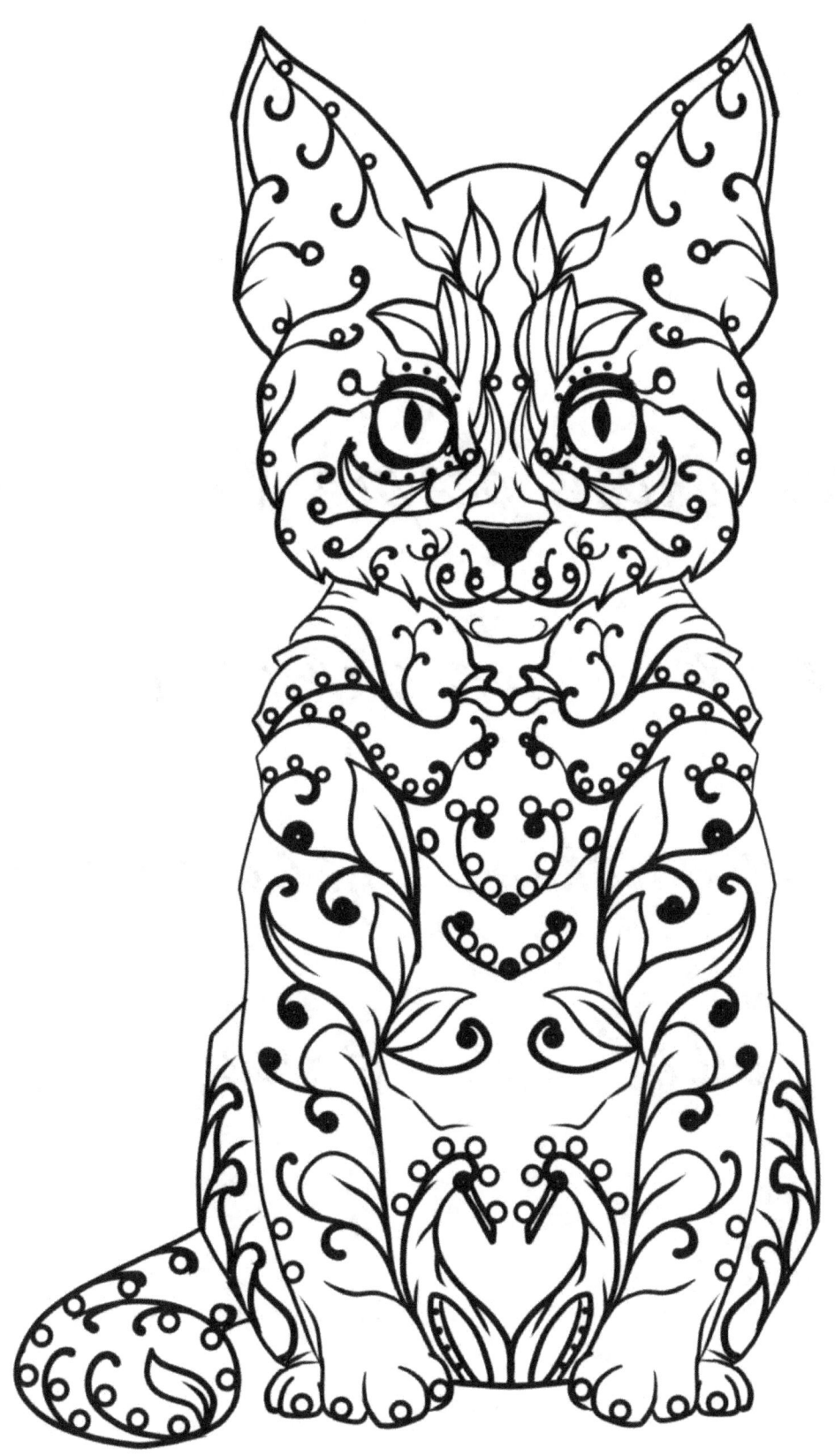

I love those people that can make me laugh during those moments when I feel like I can't even smile.

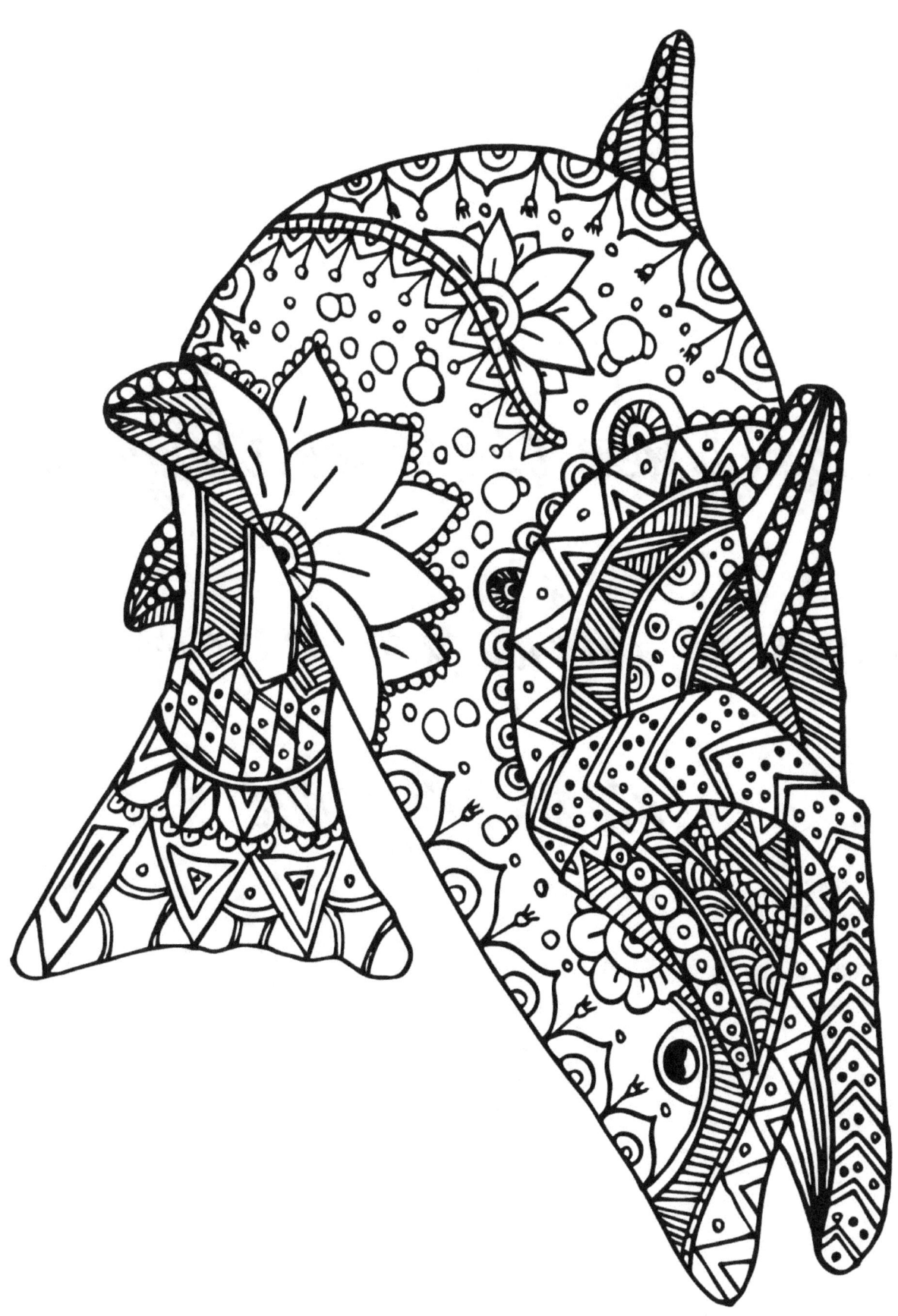

Sometimes the best thing to

do is be silent and watch how

things play out.

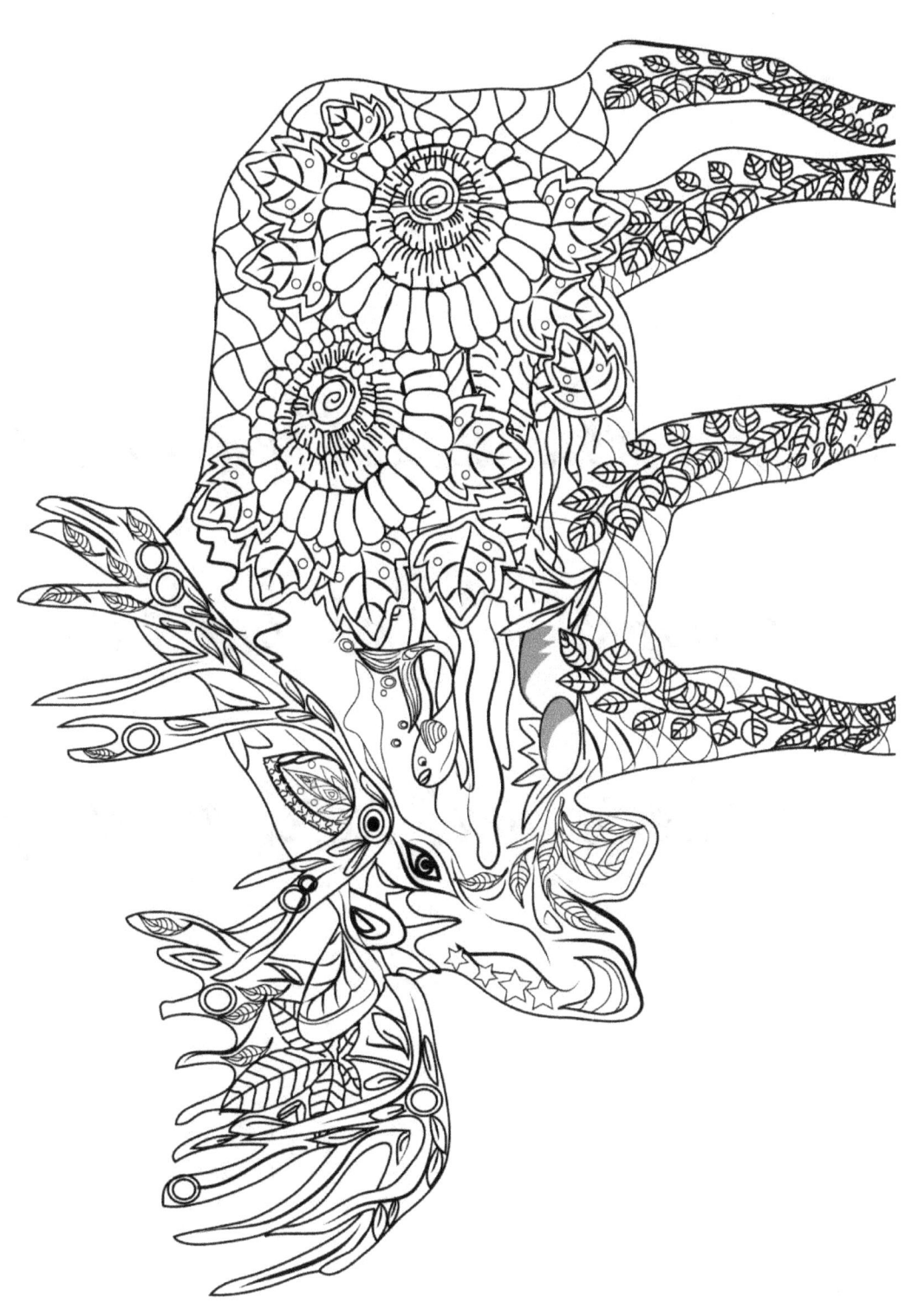

Every now and then it's good to pause in the pursuit of happiness and just be happy.

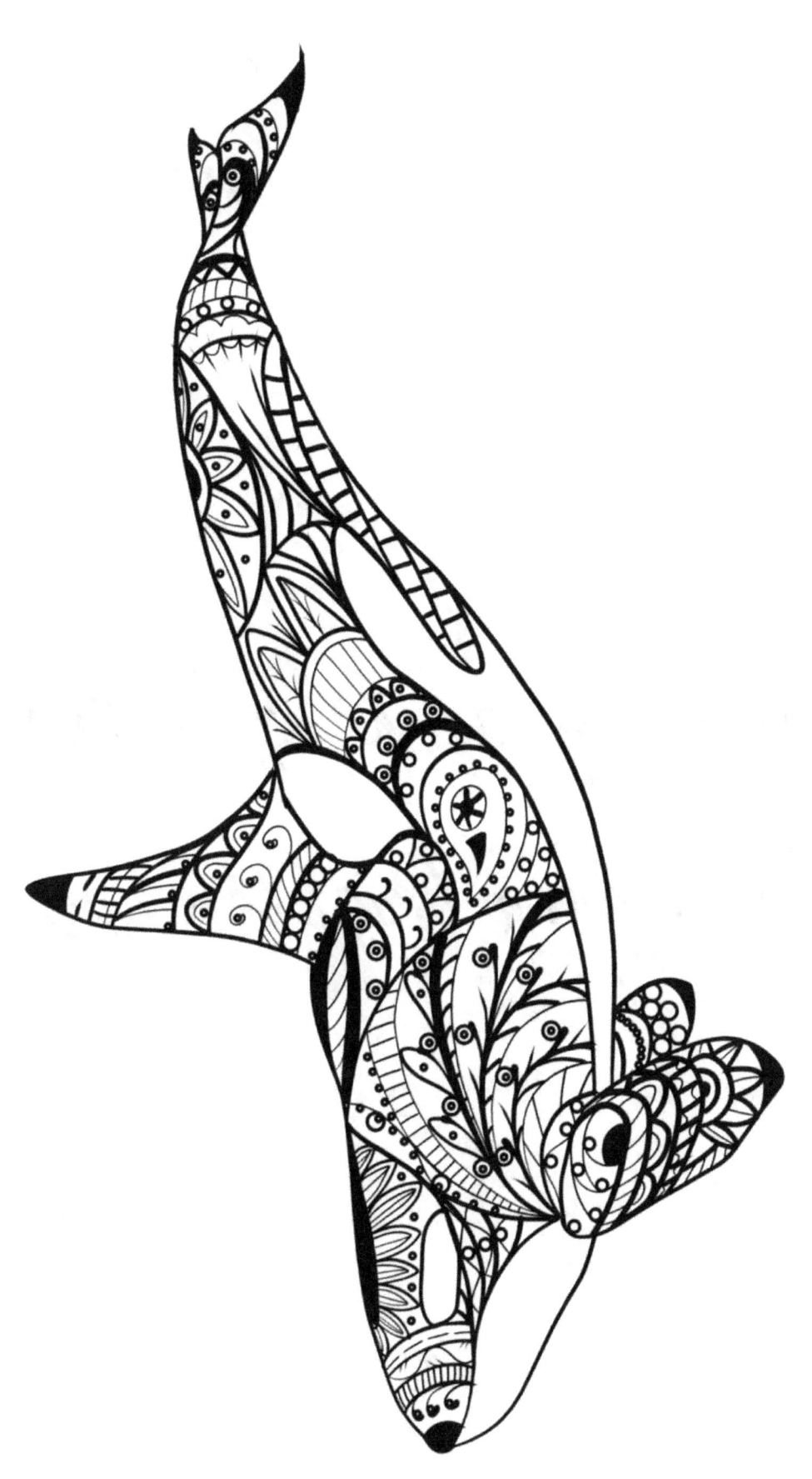

For every dark night there
is an even brighter day.

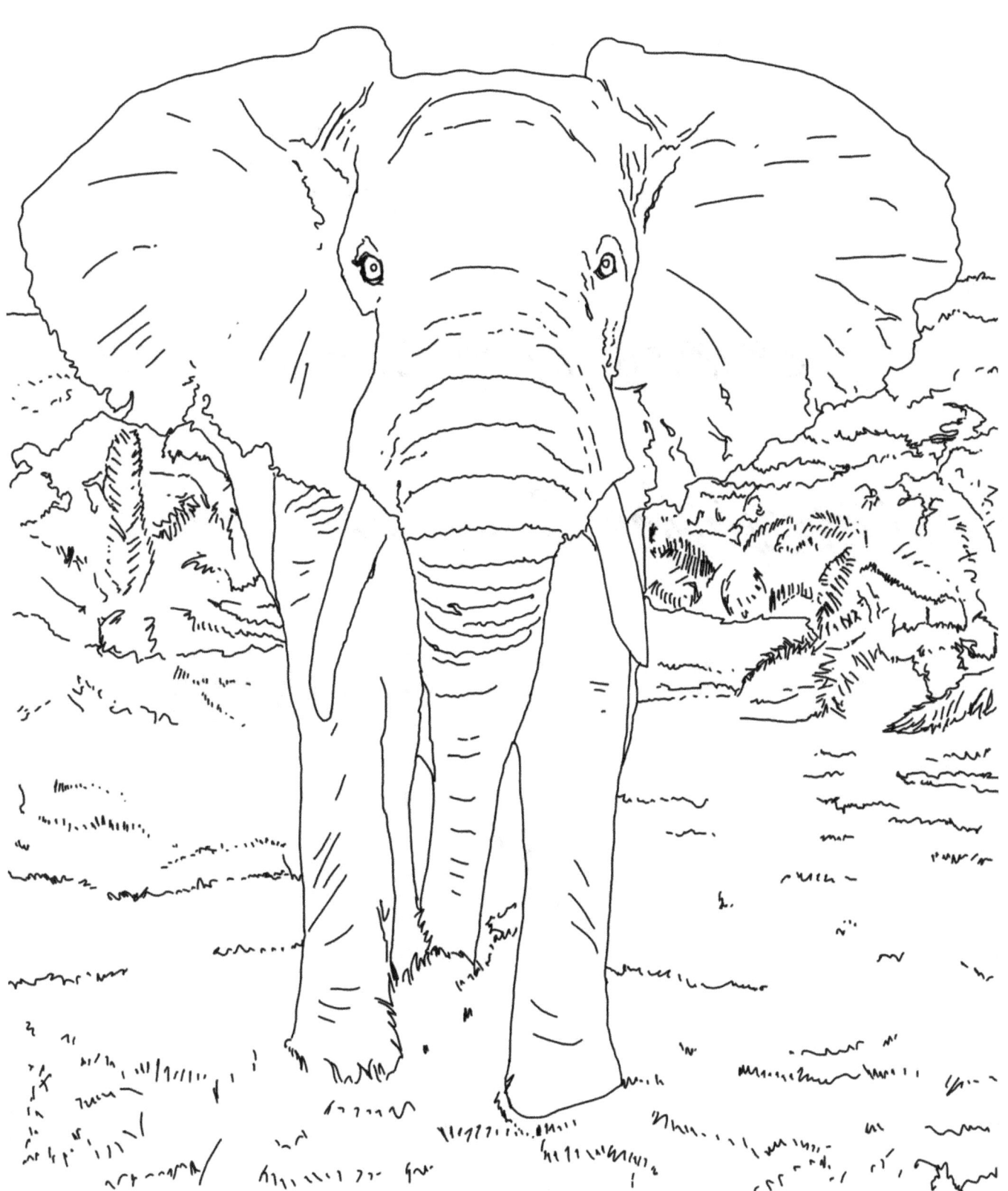

The happiest people don't necessarily have the best of everything they just make the best of everything they have.

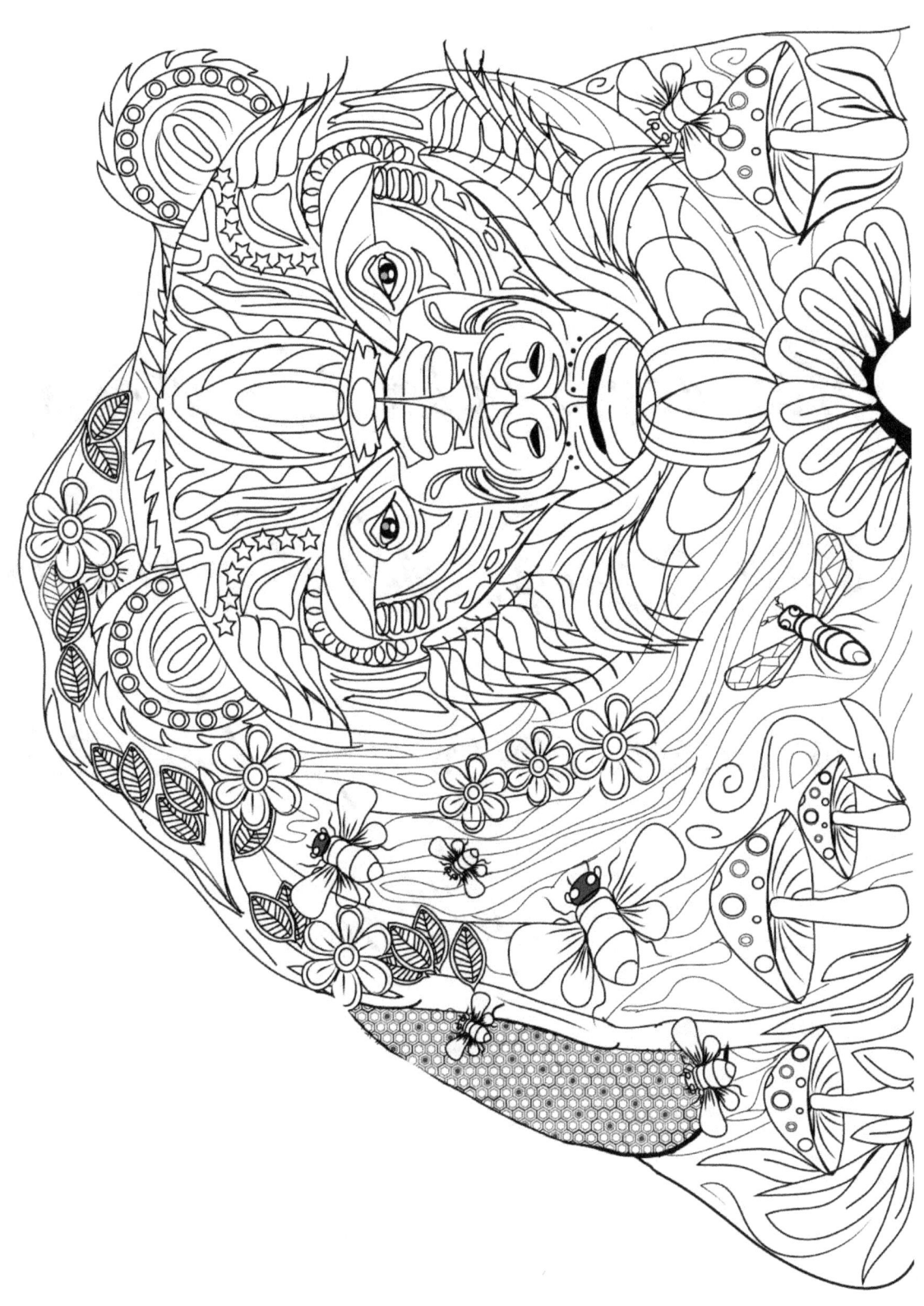

You can't calm the storm, so stop trying. What you can do is calm yourself. The storm will pass.

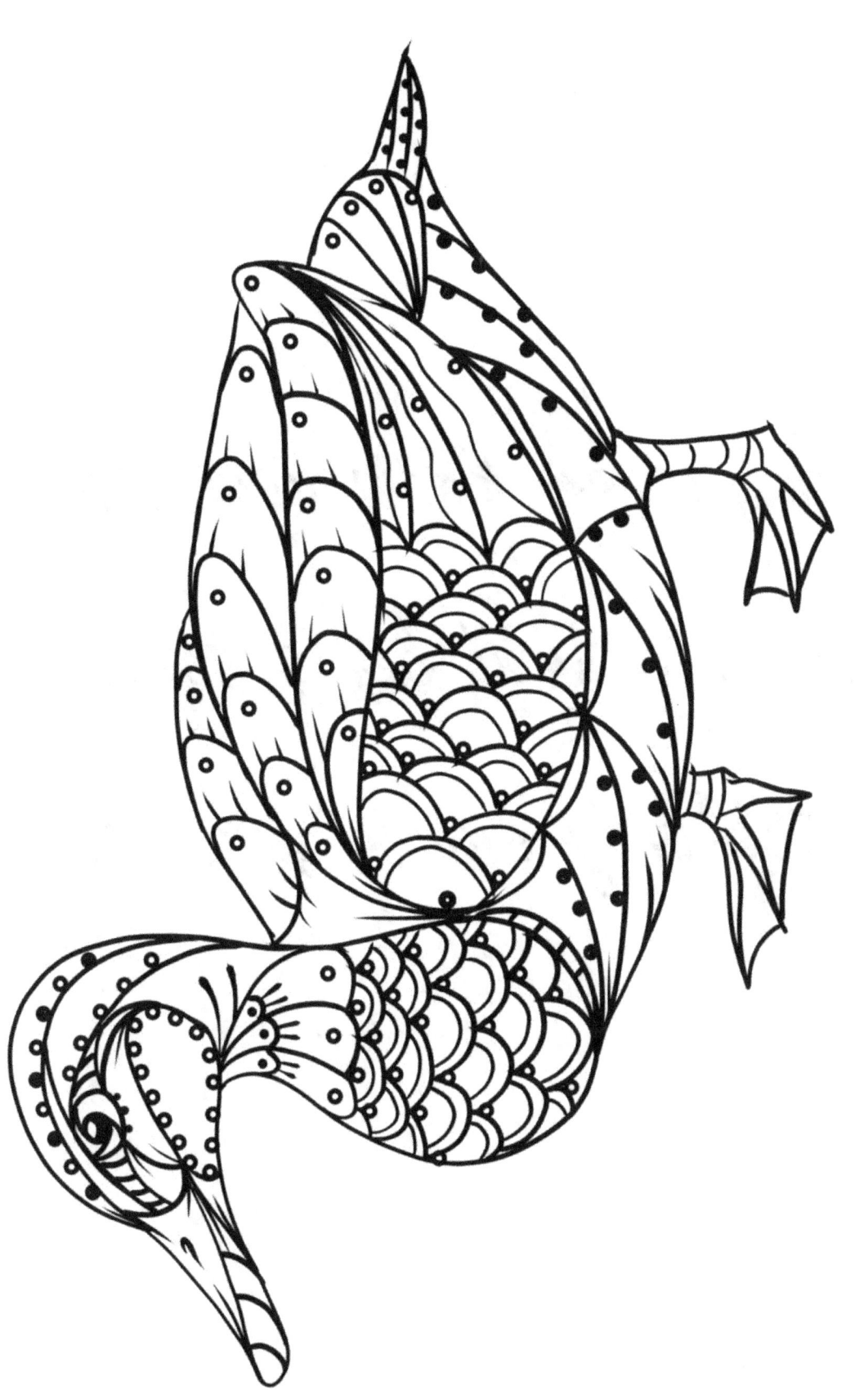

You never know how strong you are until being strong is the only choice you have.

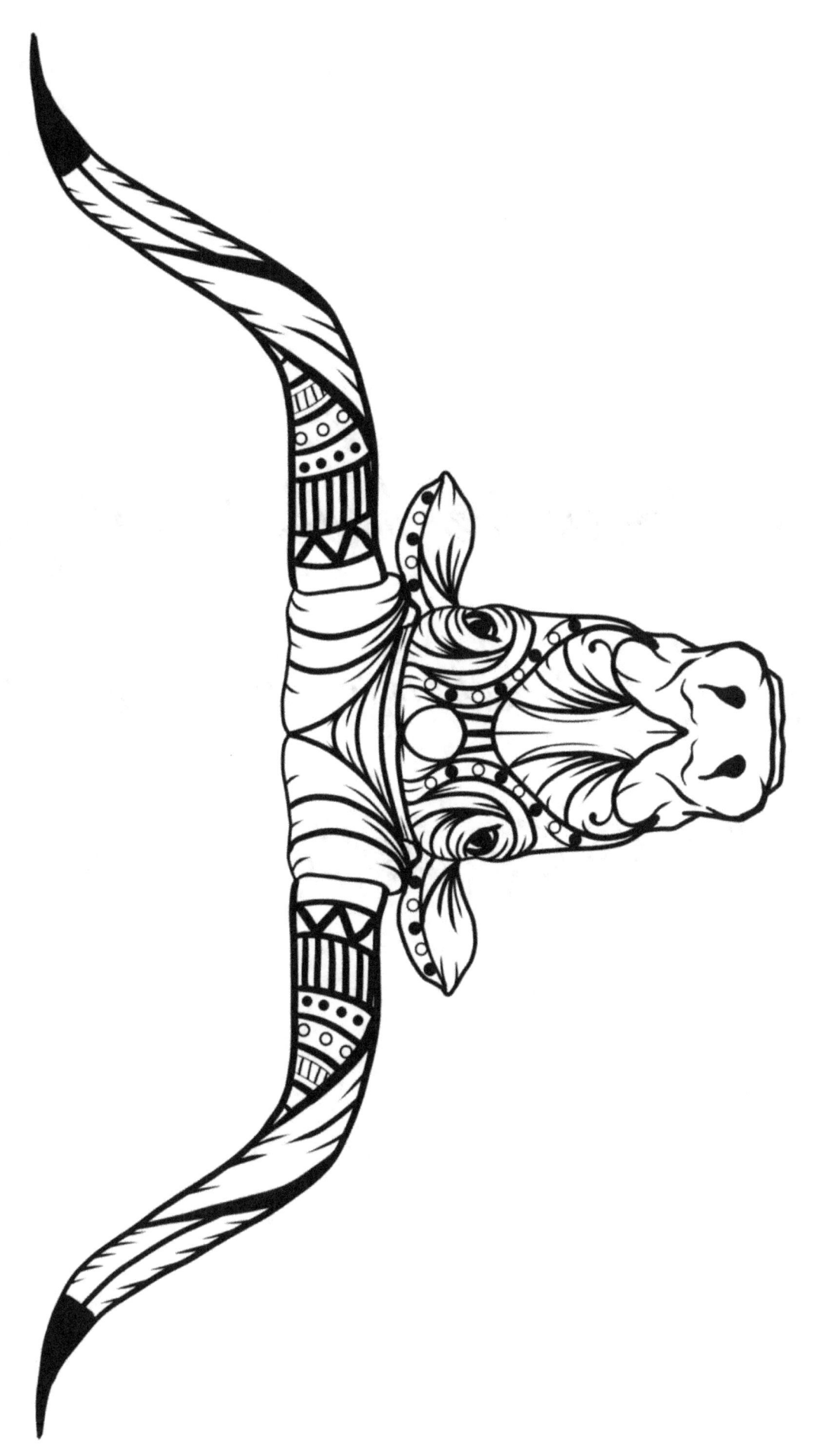

Sometimes we have to let go of what's killing us, even if it's killing us to let go.

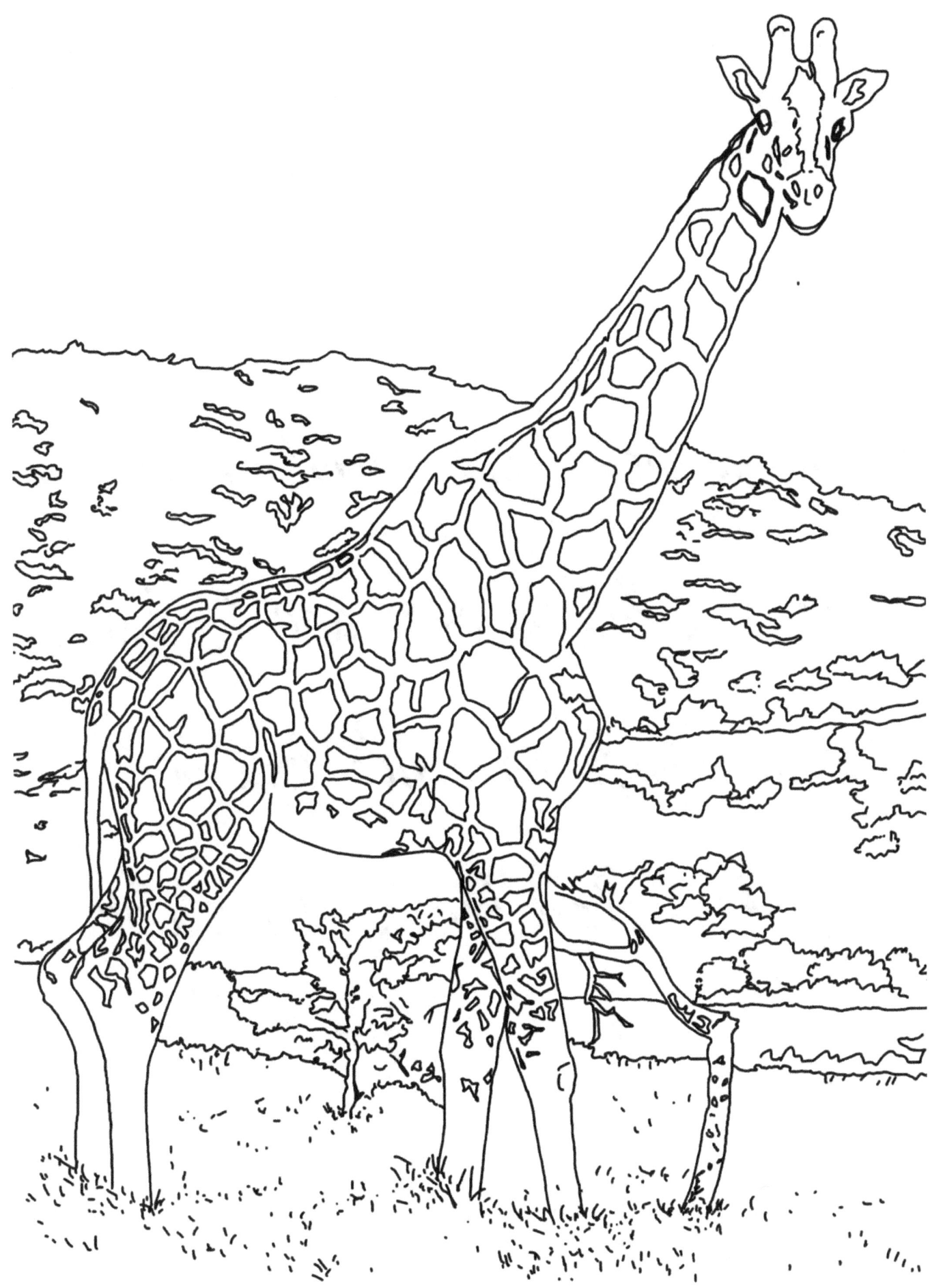

True strength is when you have a lot to cry about, but you choose to smile and take another step forward instead.

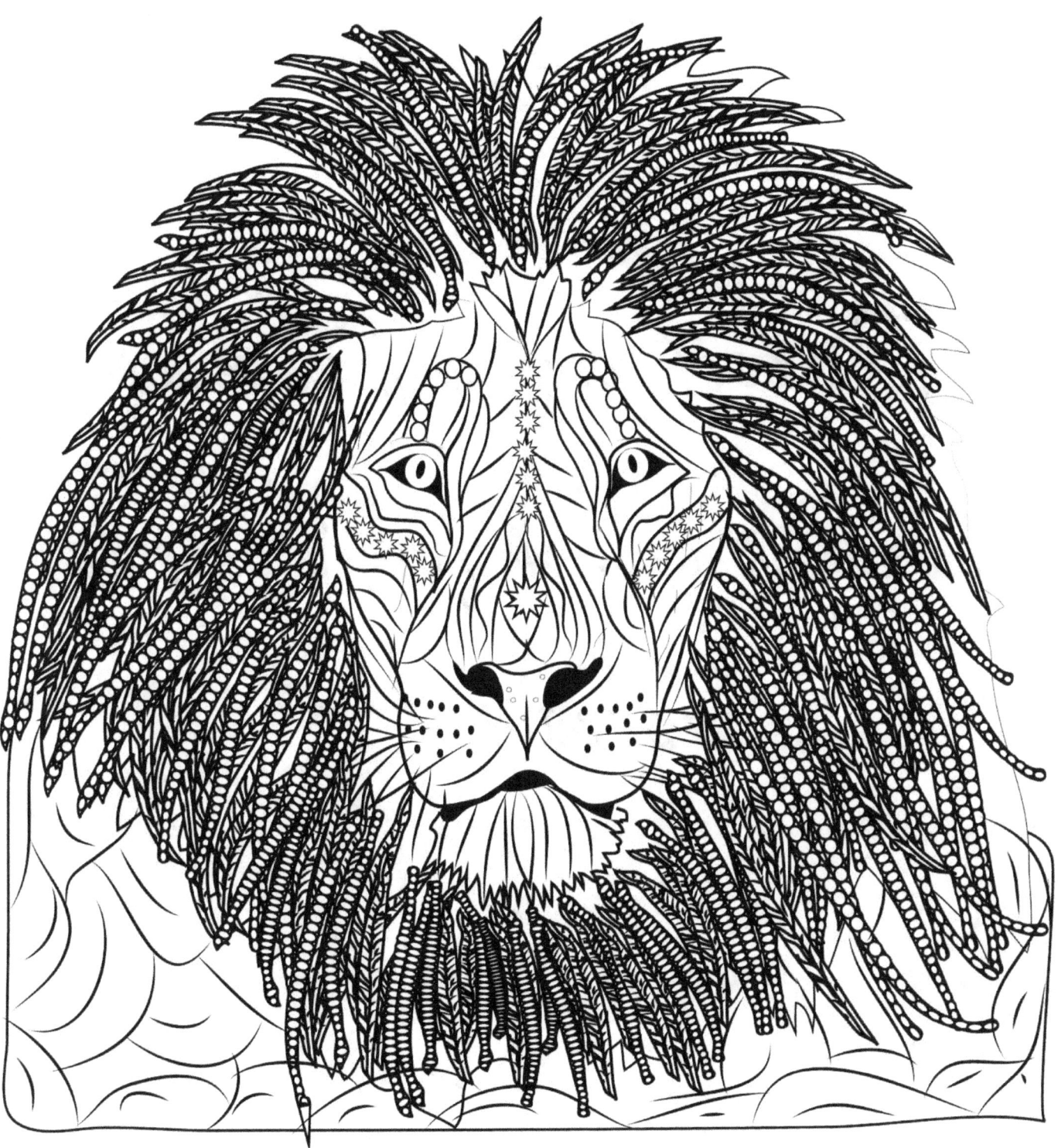

The best way to find peace

is not to search for it but, to

create it.

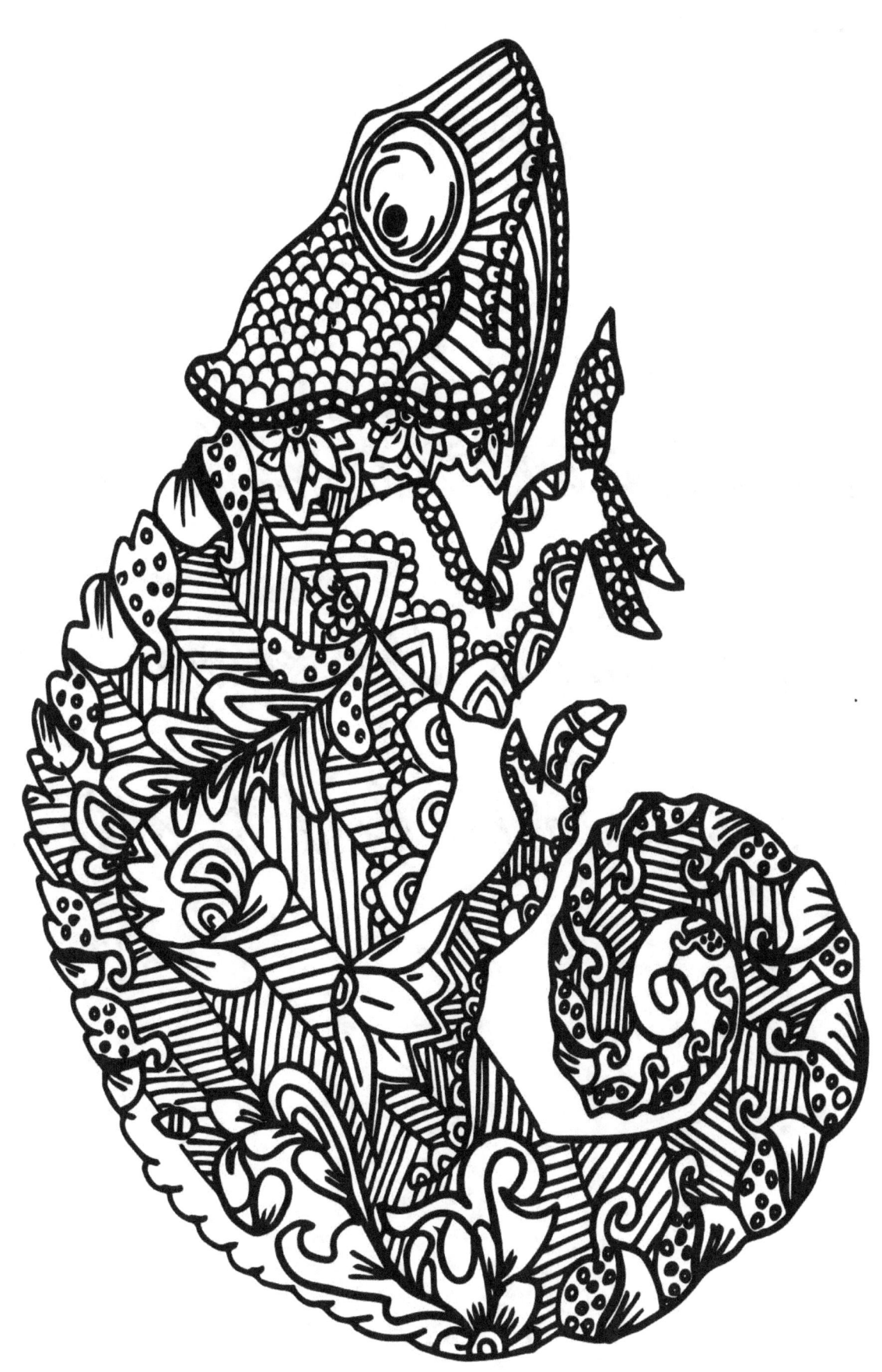

Knowing what it feels like to

be in pain is the reason why

we try to be kind to others.

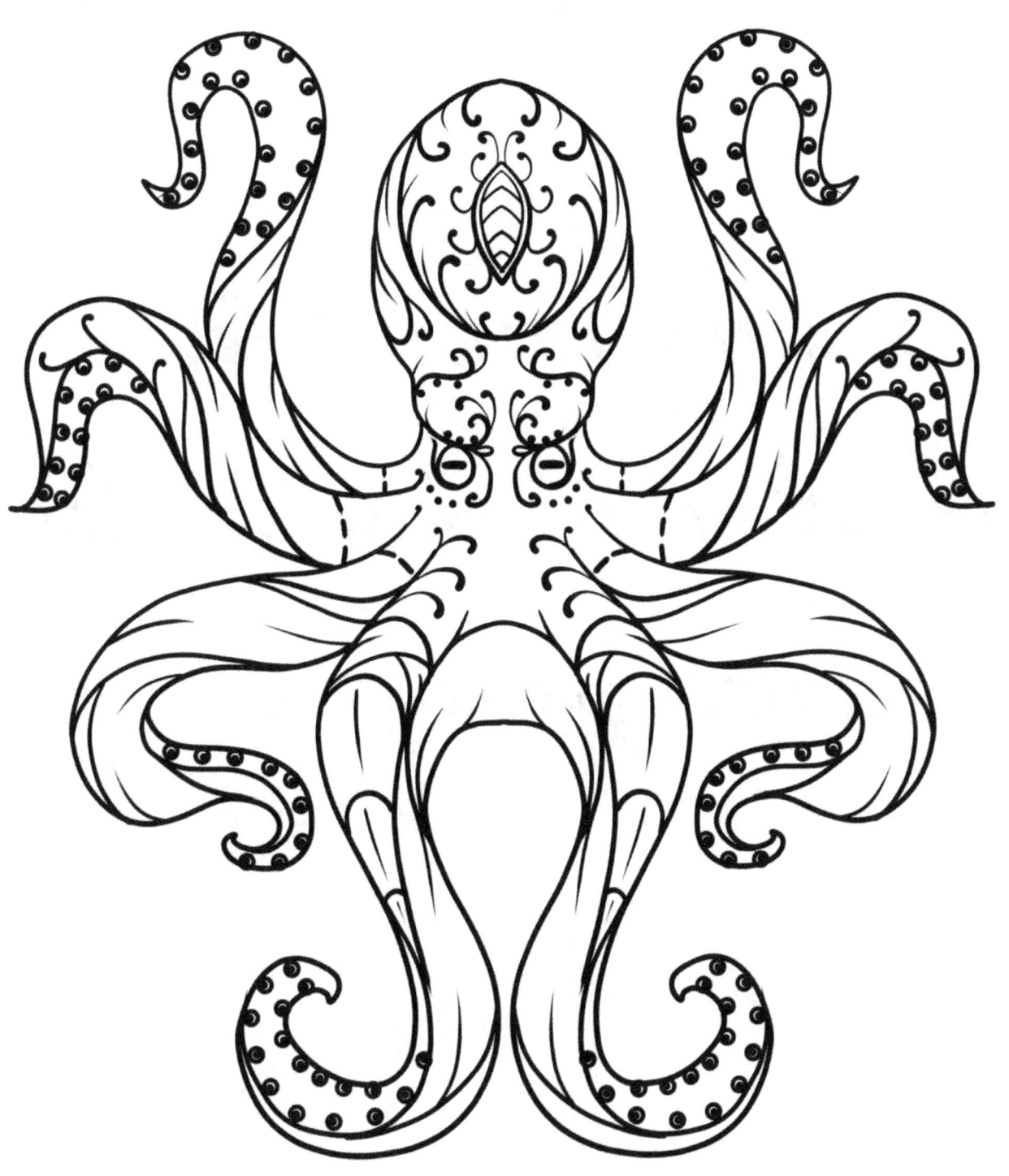

Be strong enough to let go
and patient enough to wait for
what you deserve.

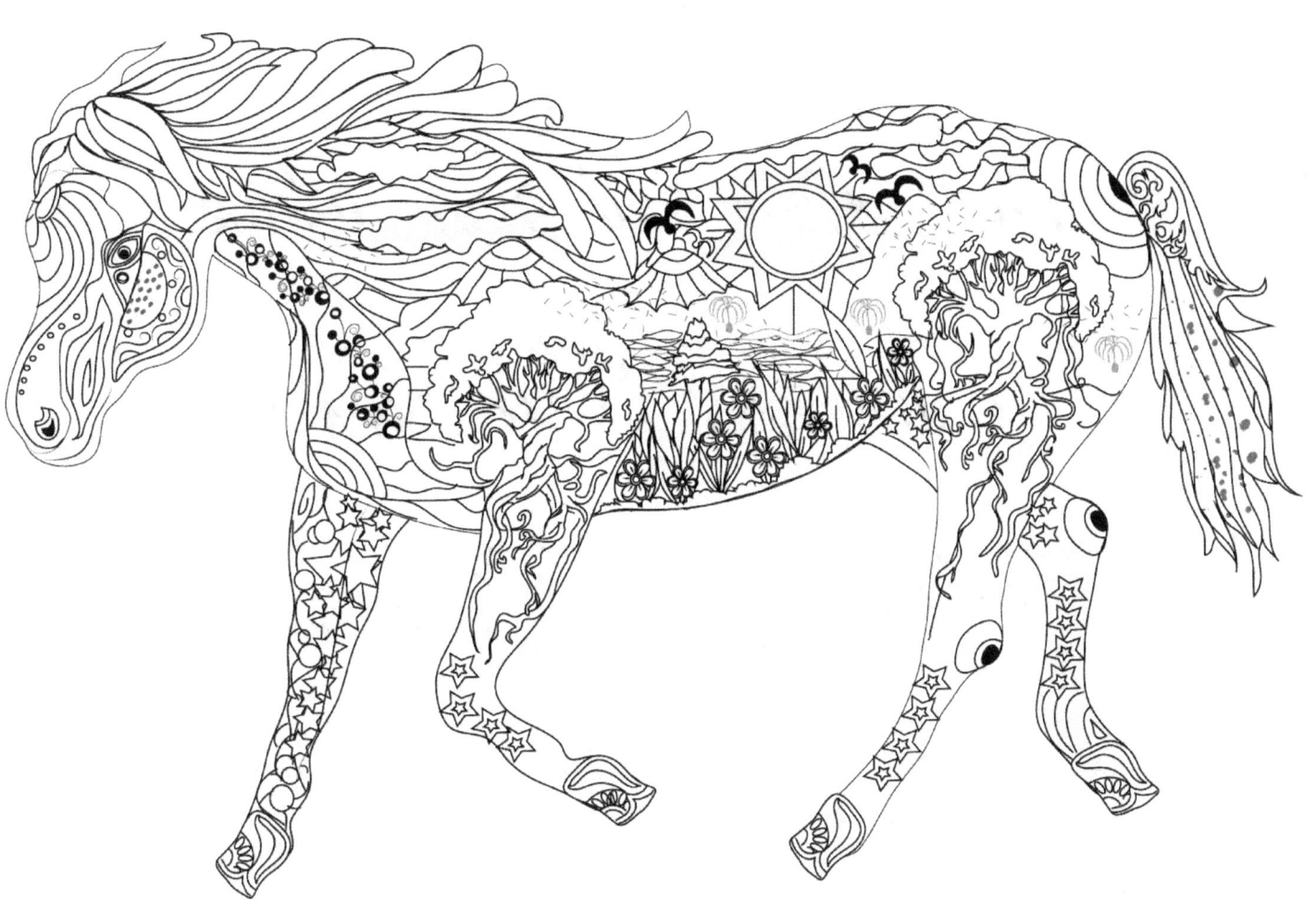

Have compassion for all beings, rich and poor alike, each has their own sufferings. ~Buddha

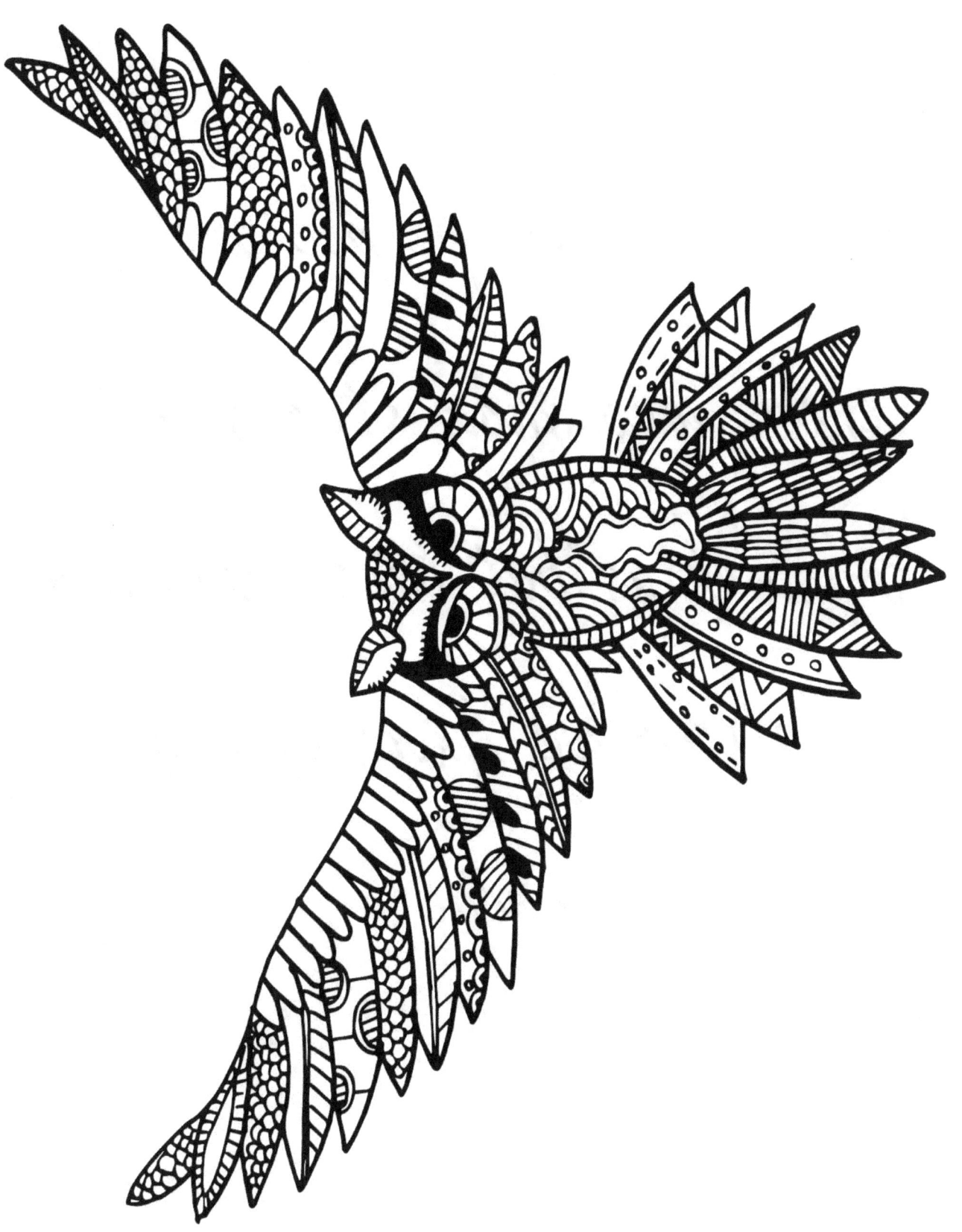

The strongest people are not those who show strength in front of us but those who win battles we know nothing about.

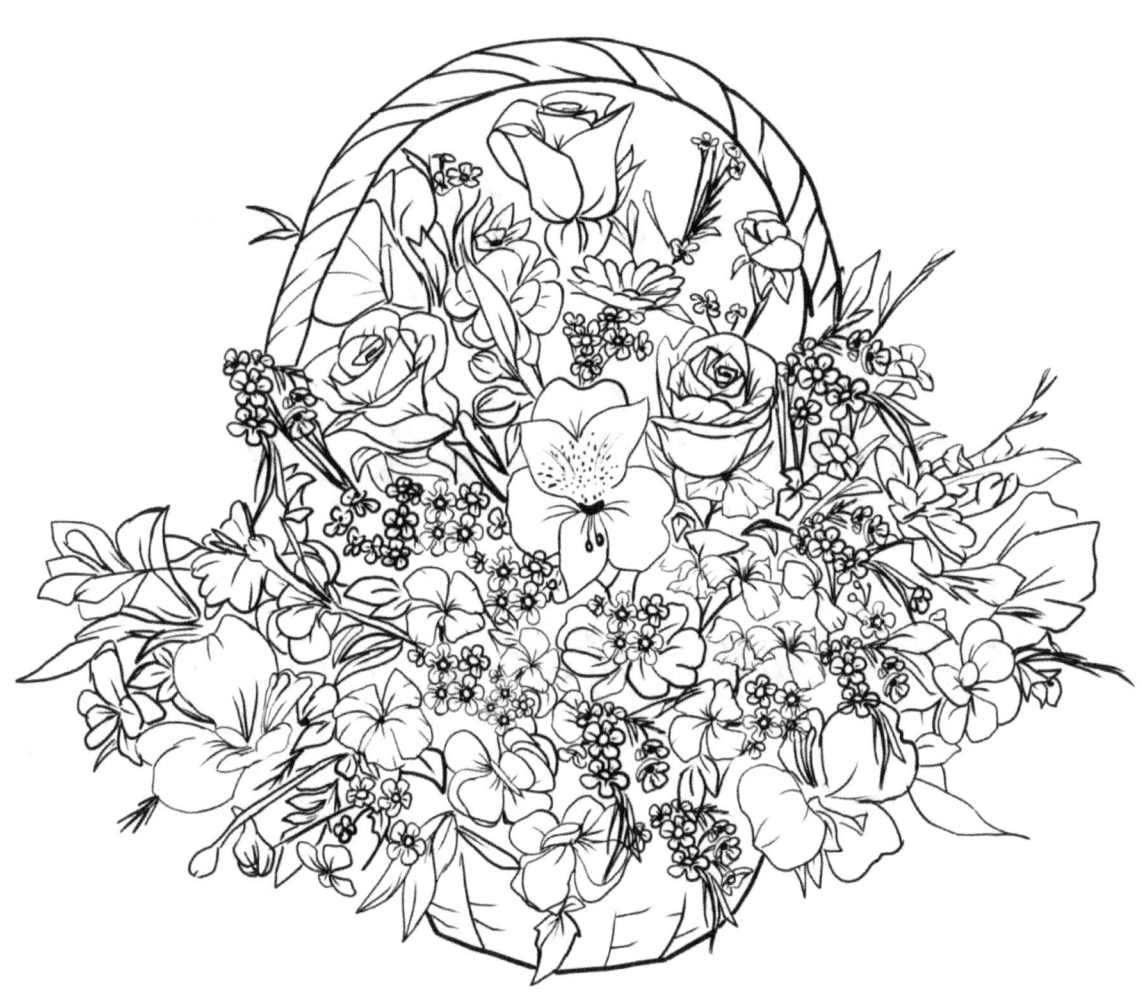

Some cause happiness

wherever they go; others

whenever they leave.

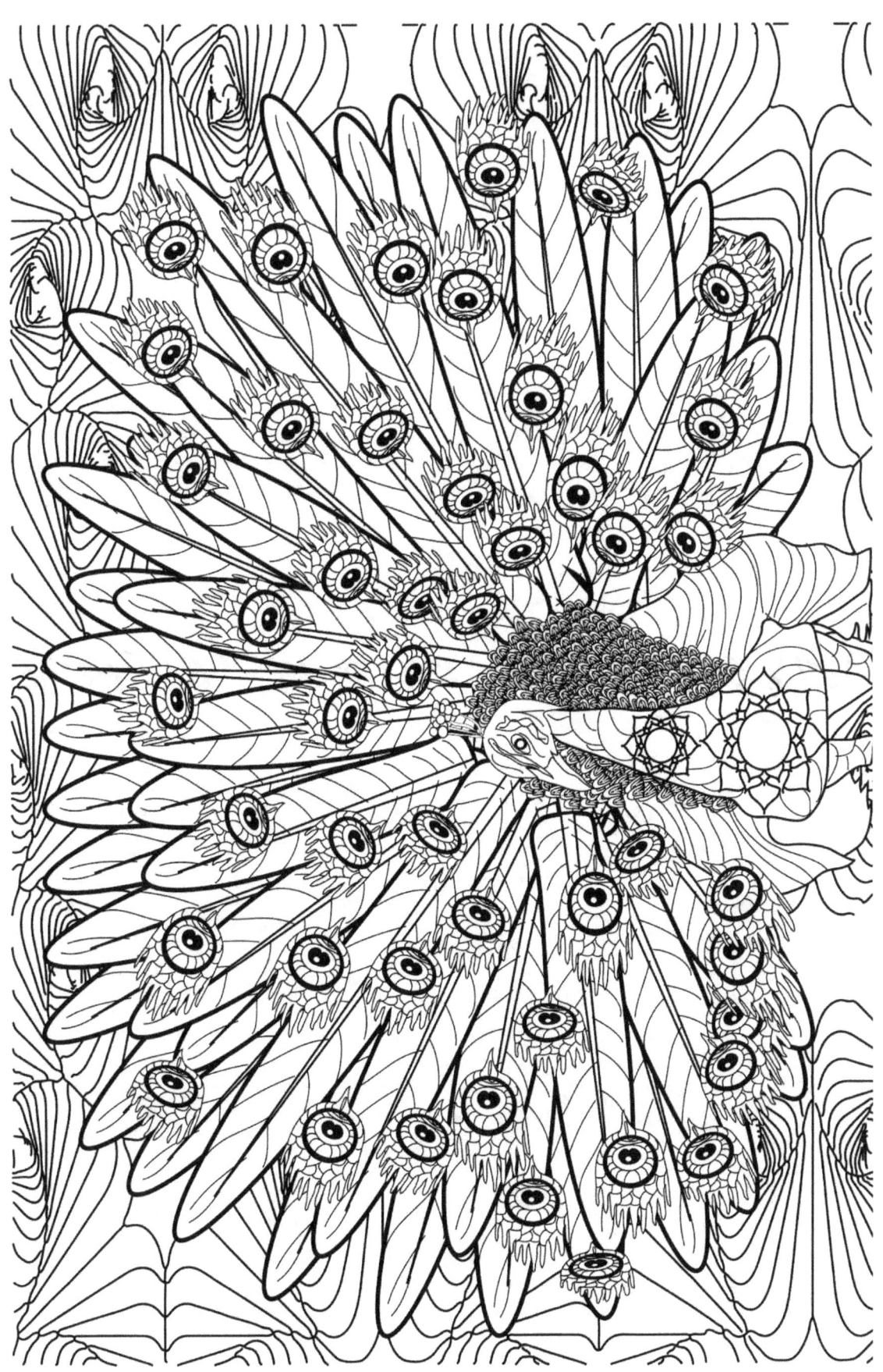

*Always find a reason to smile.*

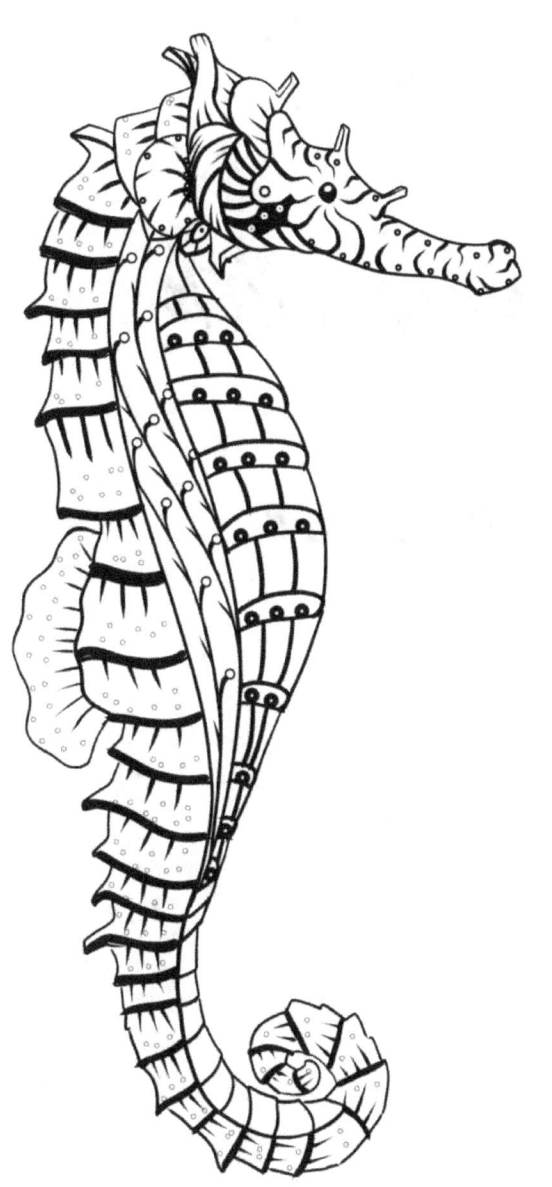 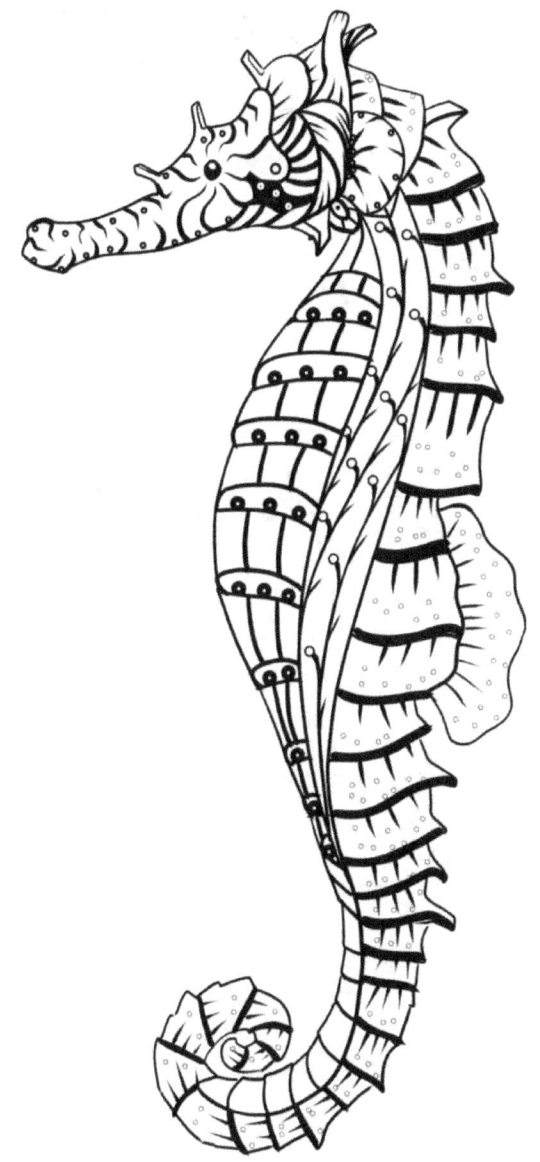

Compassion for animals is intimately connected with goodness of character.

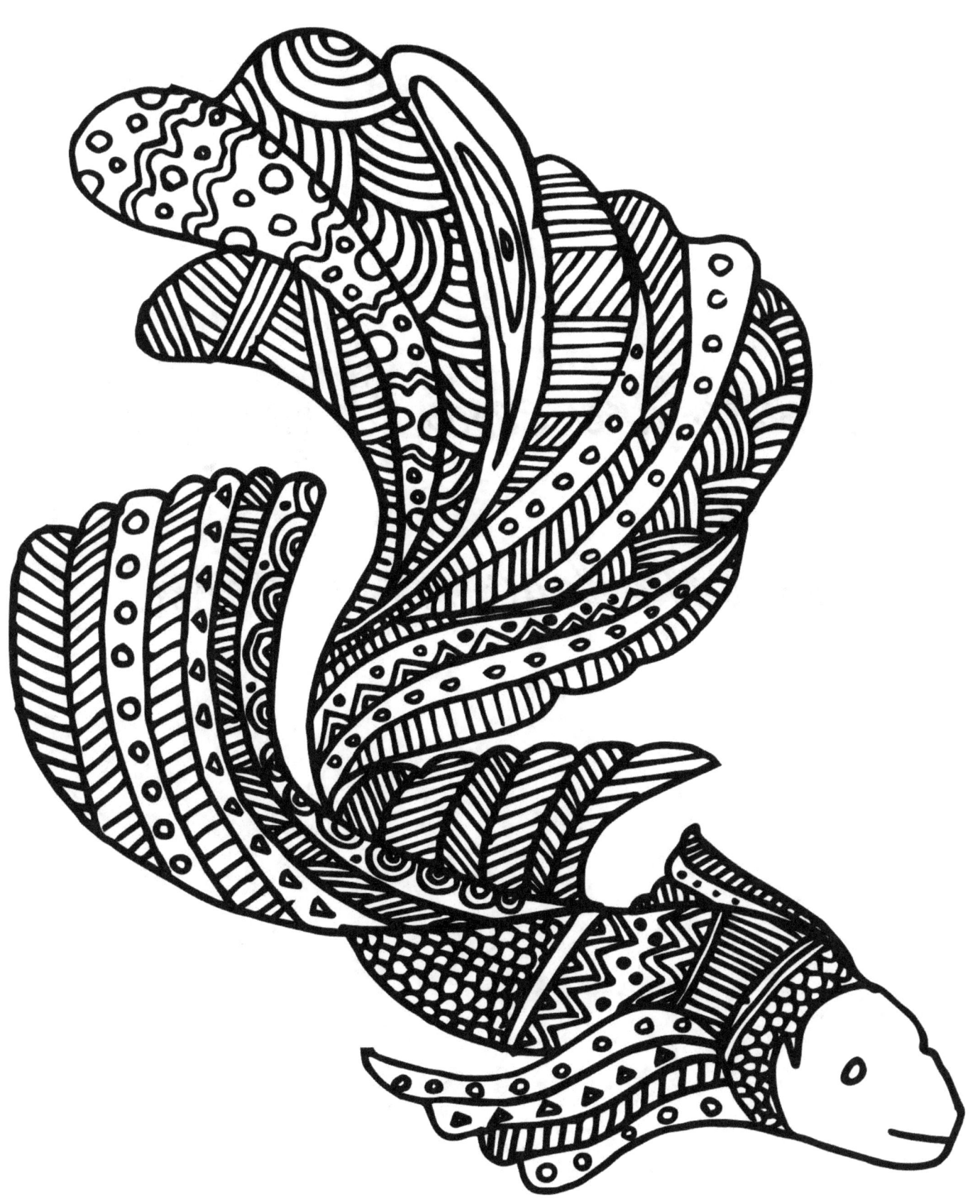

There are some things you

can only learn in a storm.

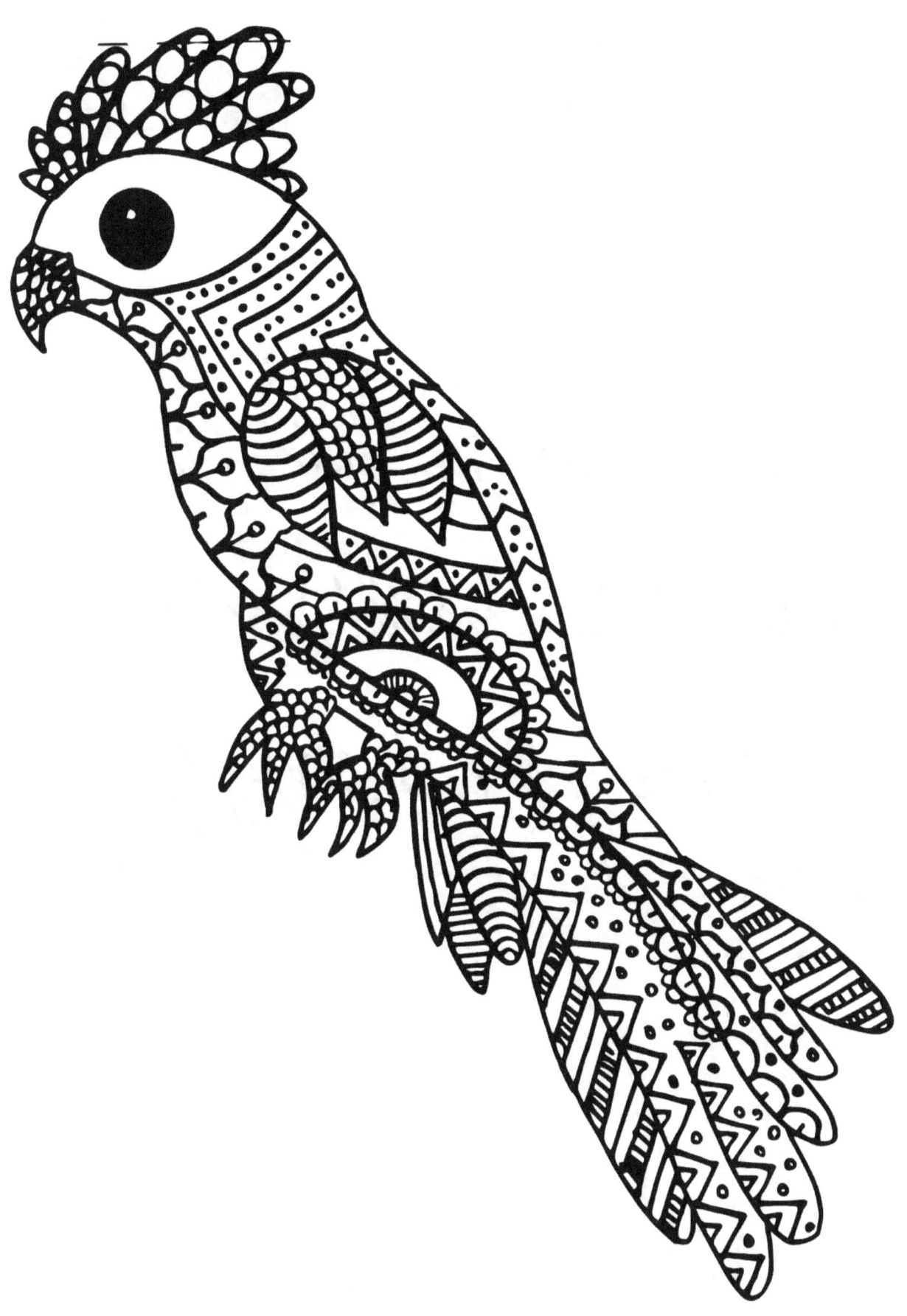

Just when the caterpillar

thought the world was over,

it became a butterfly.

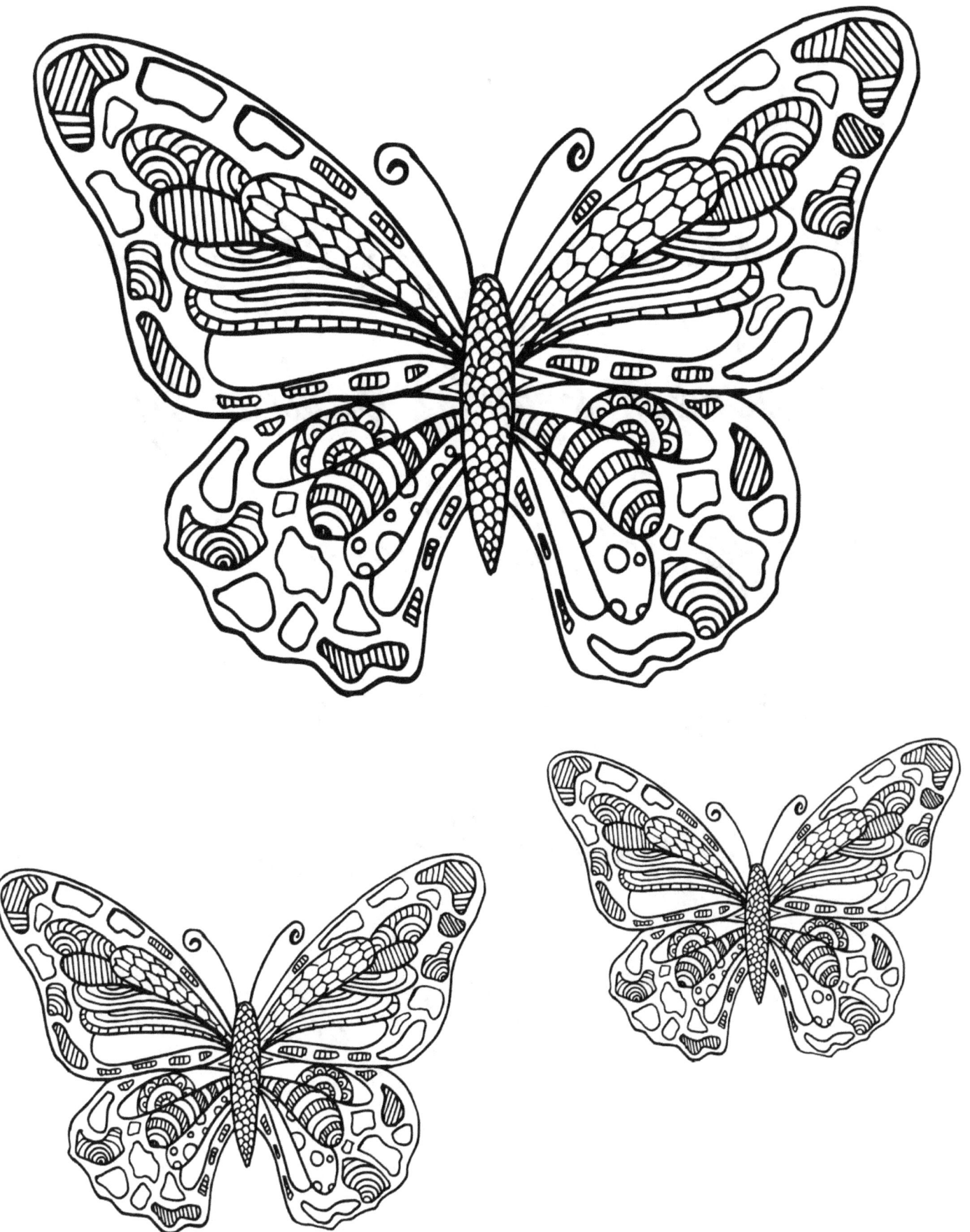

Life has many ways of testing a person's will, either by having nothing happen at all or by having everything happen all at once.

~ Paulo Coelho

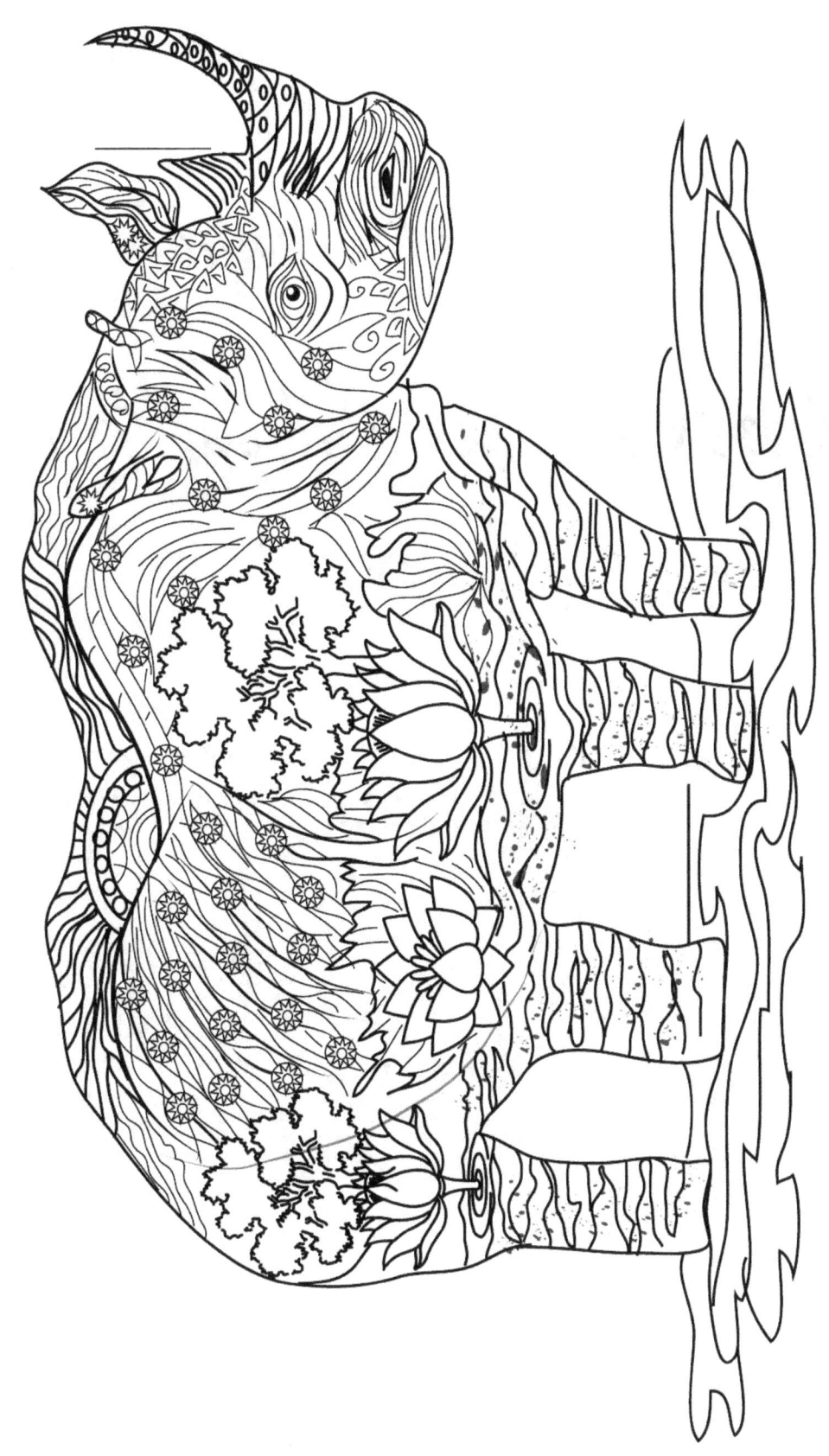

The greatest weapon against stress is the ability to choose one thought over another.
~ William James

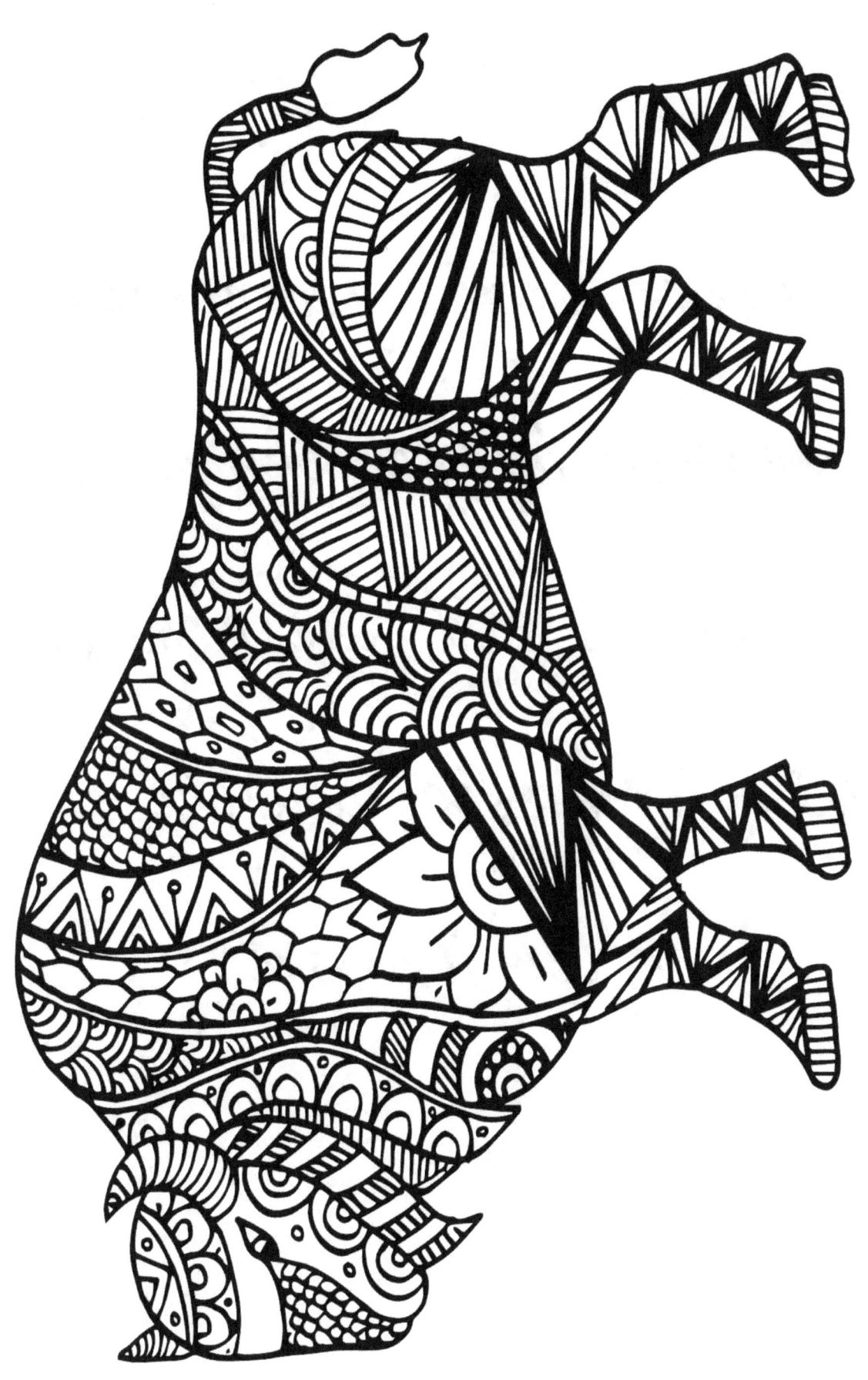

Three things you cannot recover in life: the word after its said, the moment after its missed, and the time after its gone.

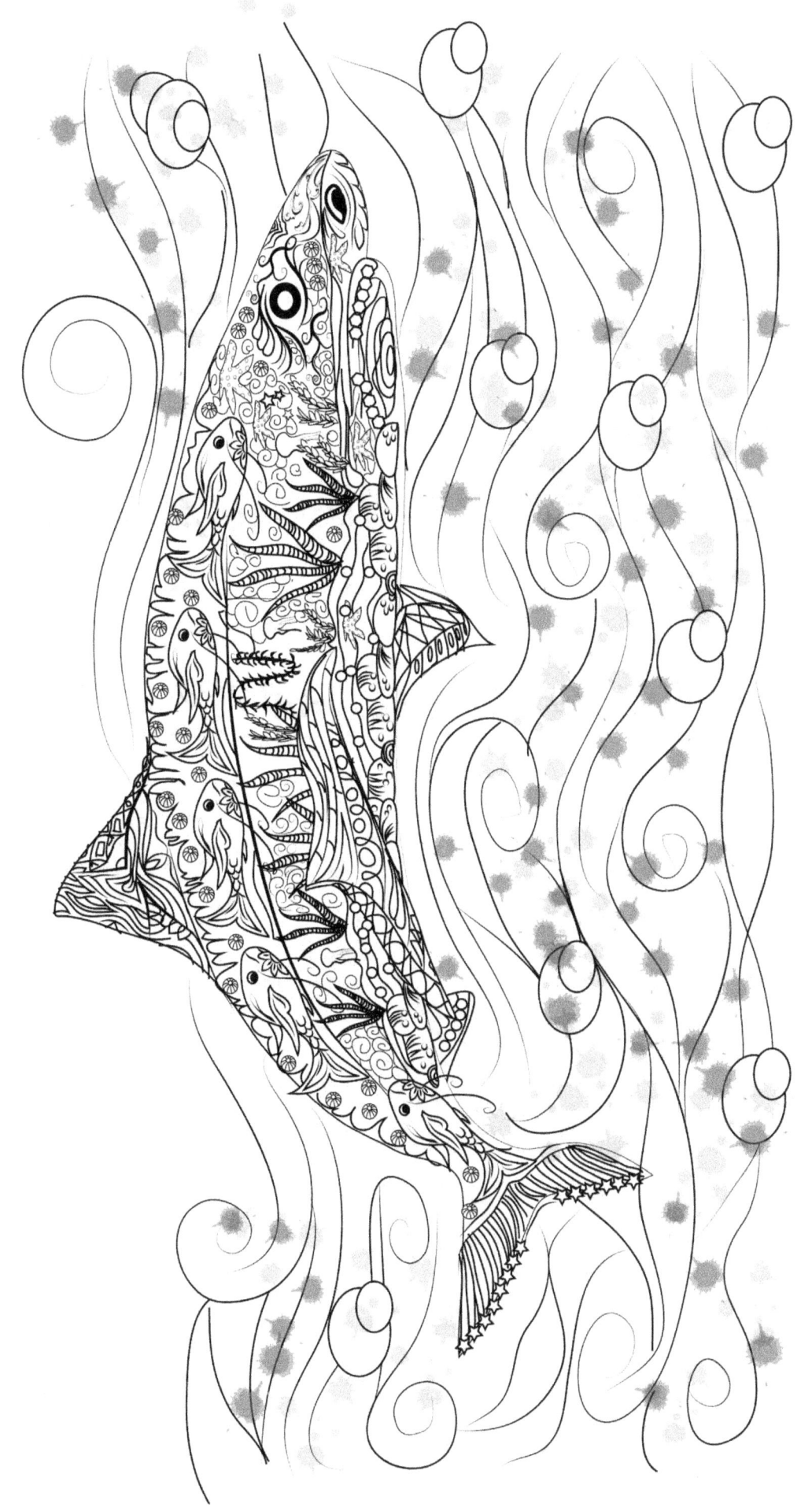

I am not what happened to me,

I am what I choose to become.

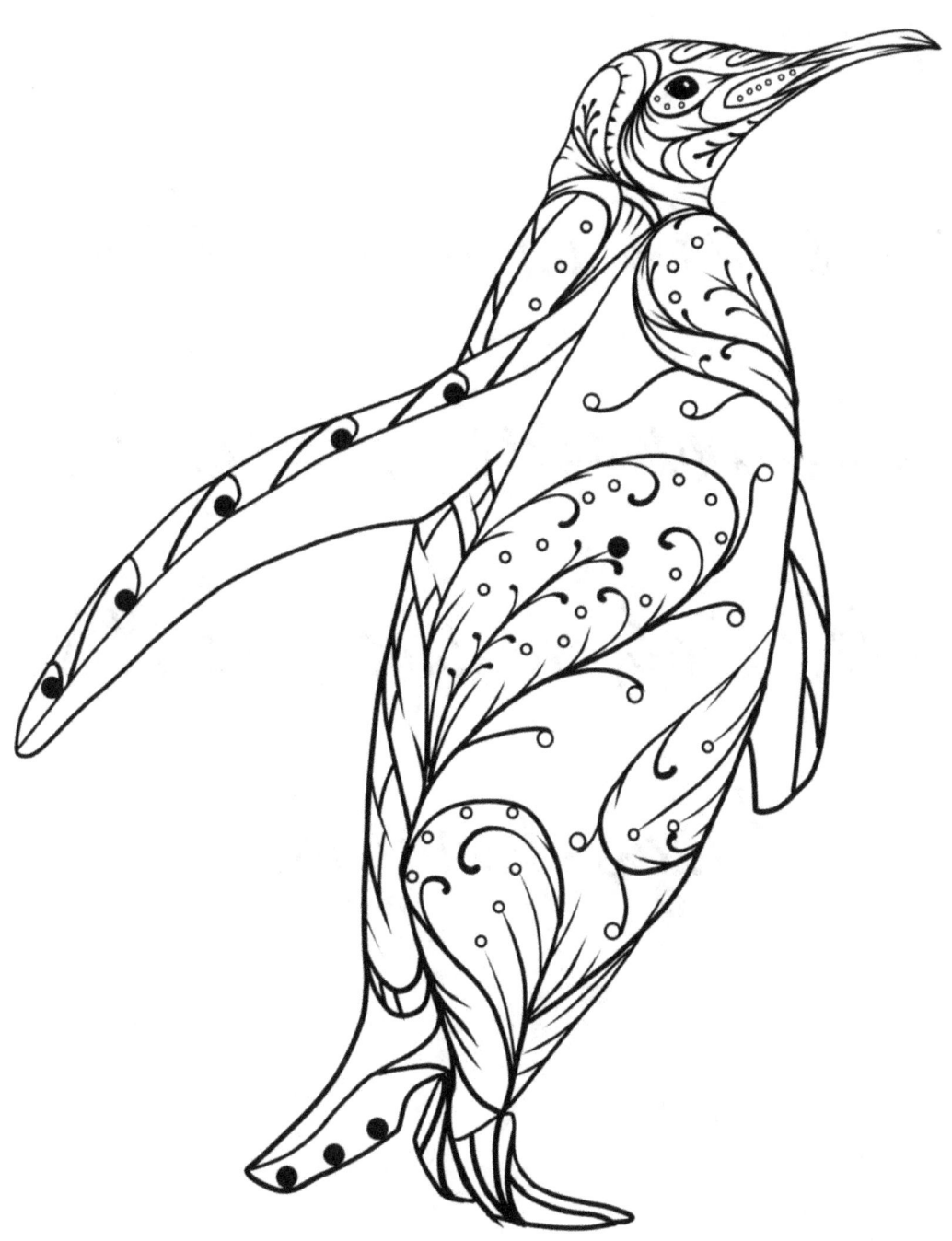

Life is like an ocean. It can be calm and still or rough and rigid. But, in the end it's always beautiful.

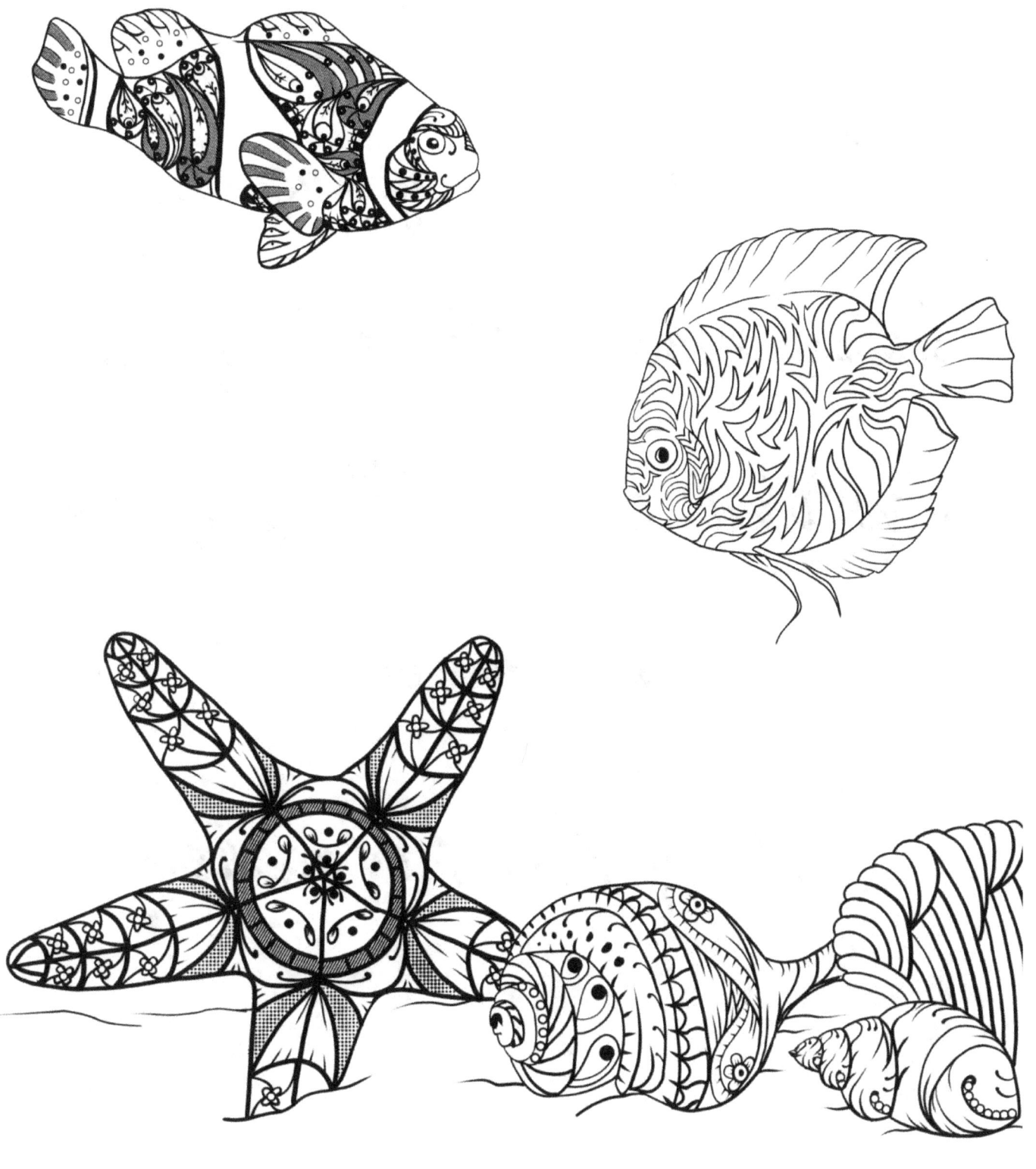

Sometimes courage is the little voice at the end of the day that says, *I'll try again tomorrow.*

~ Mary Ann Radmacher

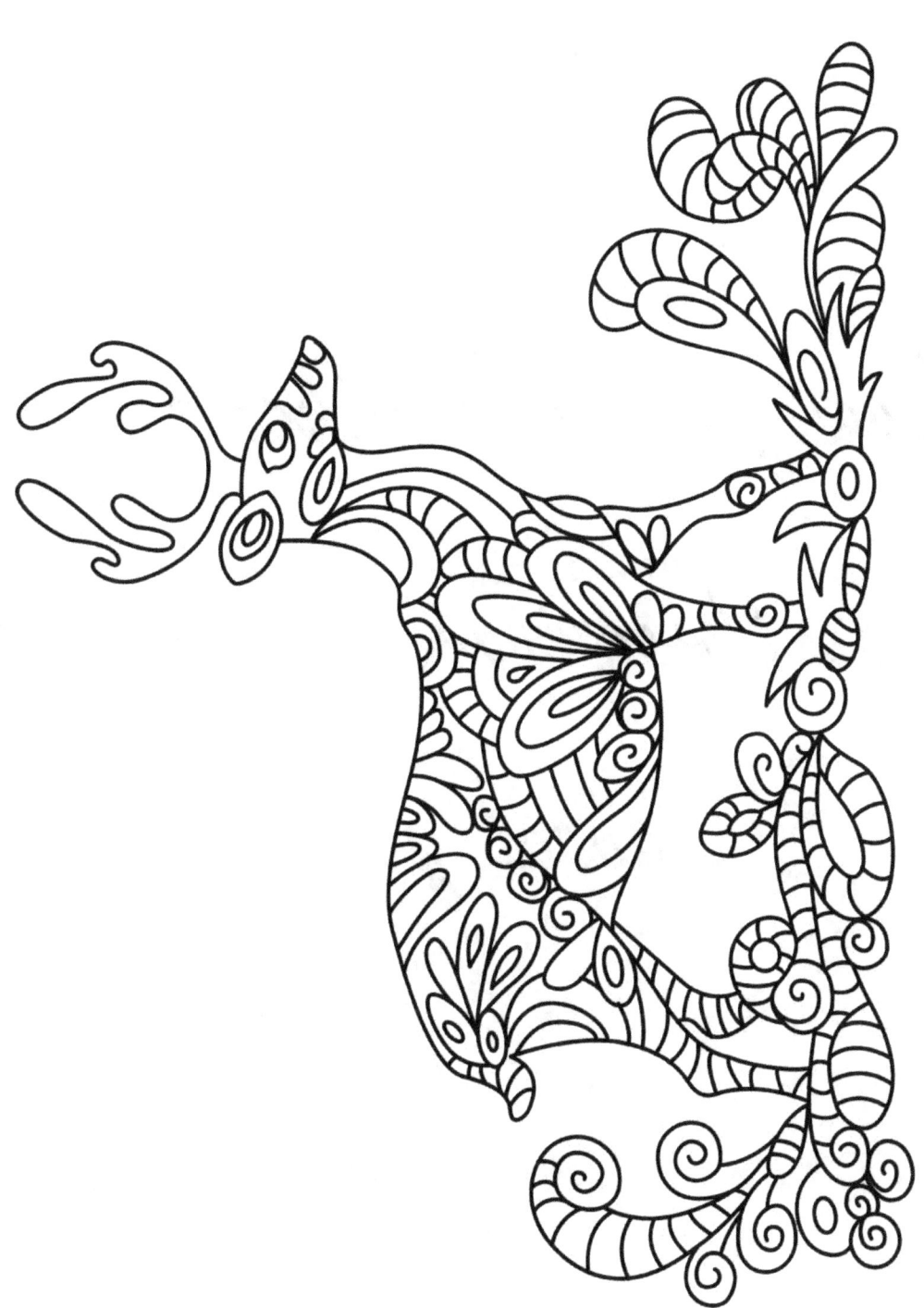

How you make others feel about themselves, says a lot about you.

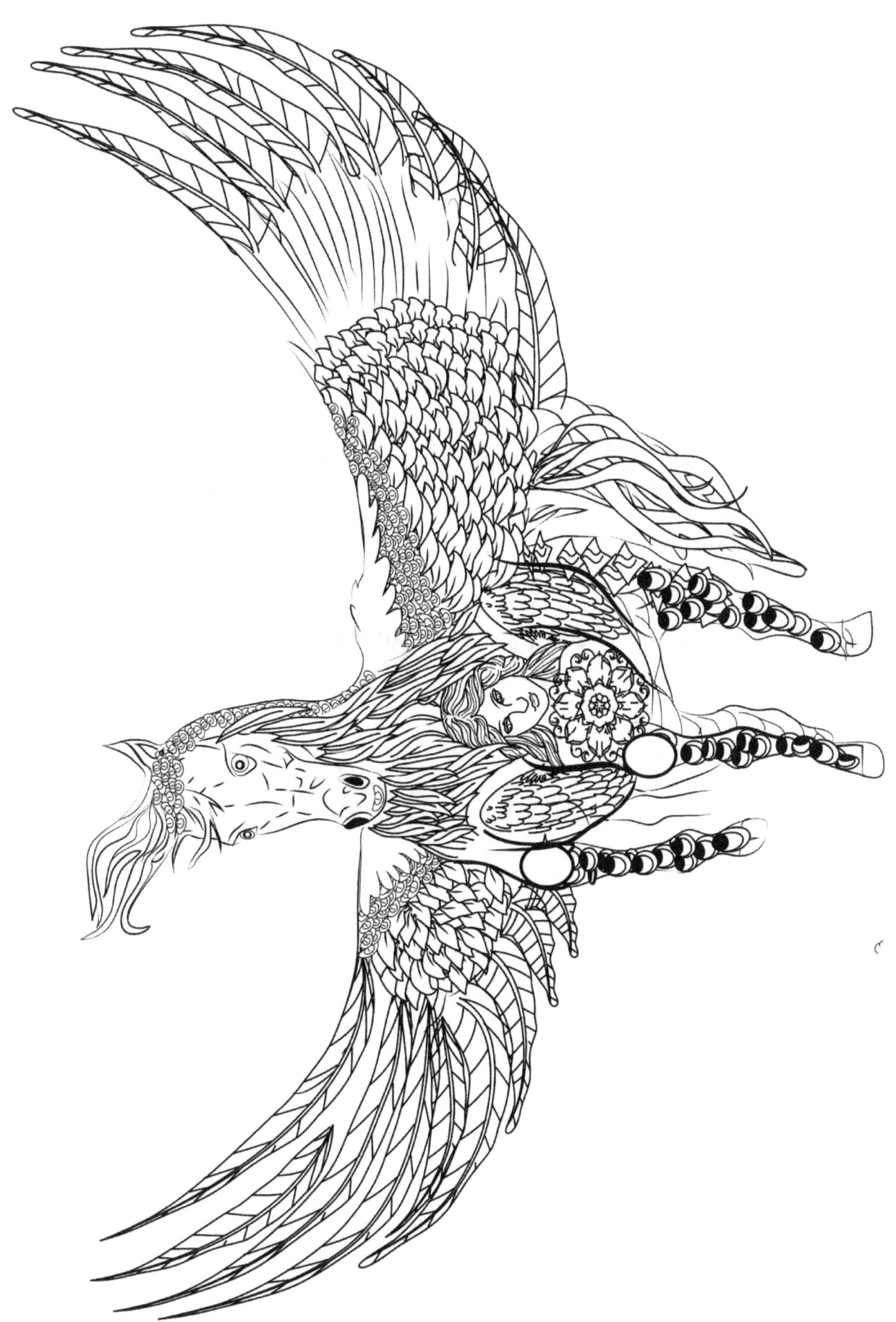

When you make a mistake

don't treat yourself like you

are the mistake.

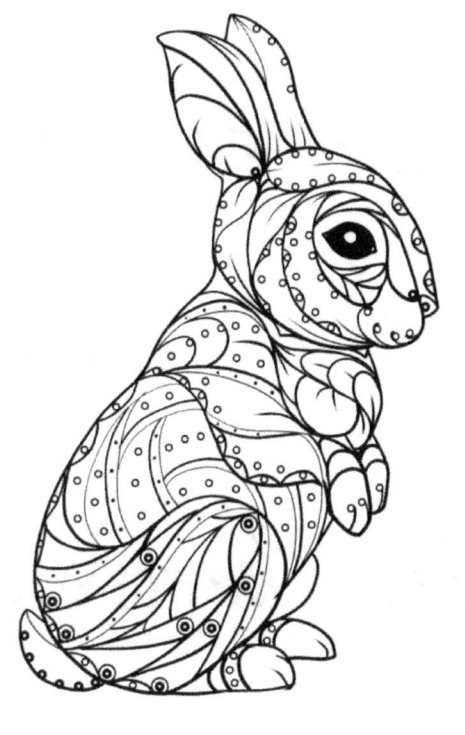
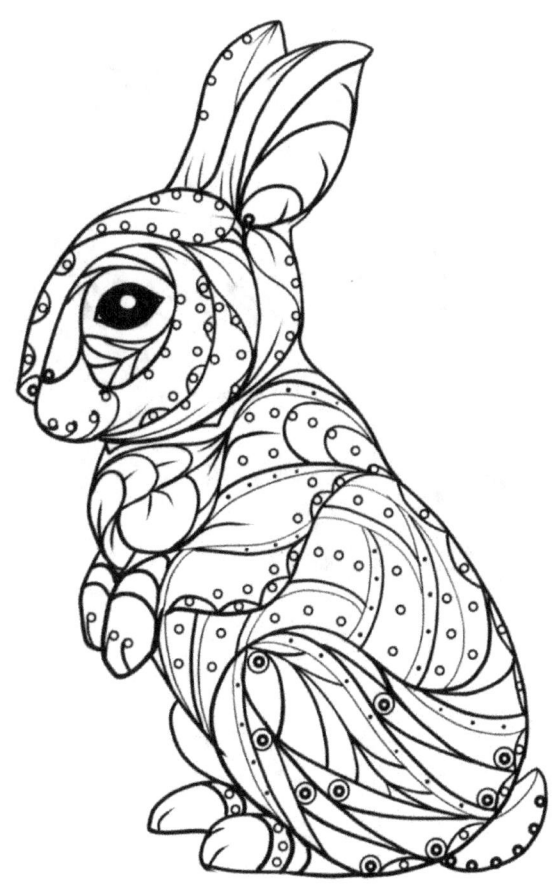
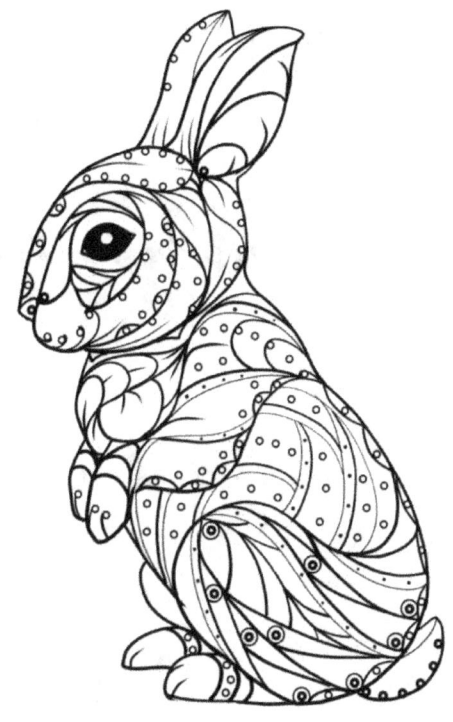

If you've got a dream you need to protect it. People can't do something themselves, they want to tell you that you can't do it. You want something, get it period.

~ Will Smith

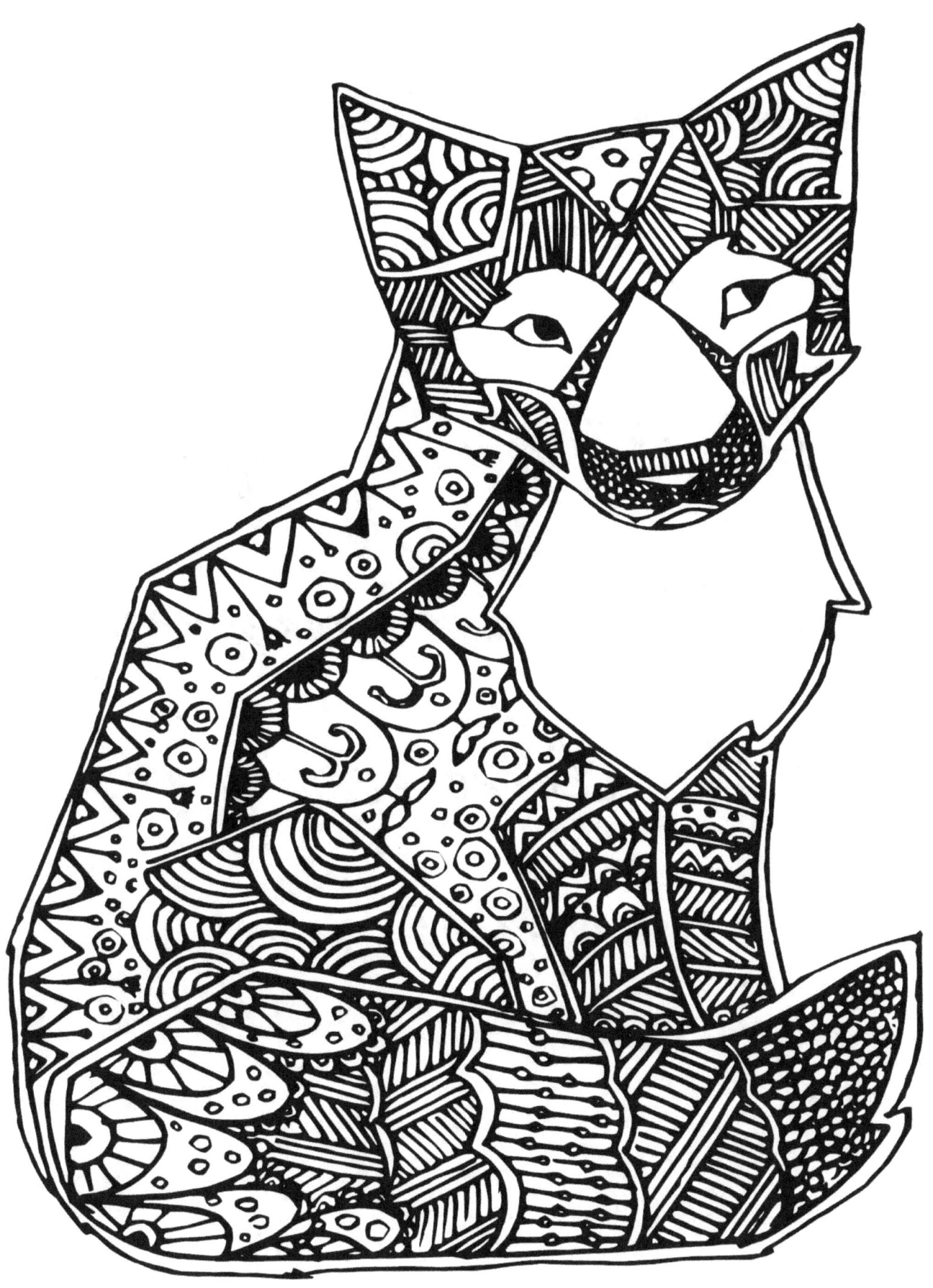

The ability to simplify is
to eliminate the unnecessary
so that the necessary may
speak.

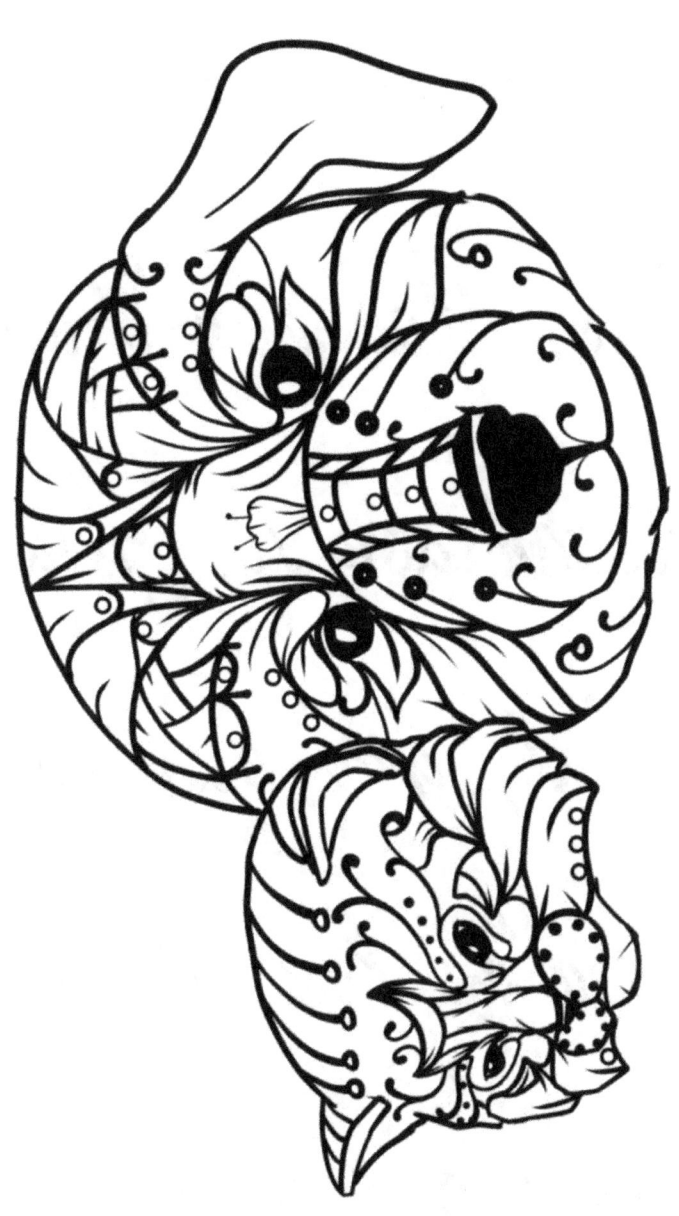

Time is free, but it's priceless. You can't own it, but you can use it. You can't keep it but, you can spend it. Once you've lost it you can never get it back.

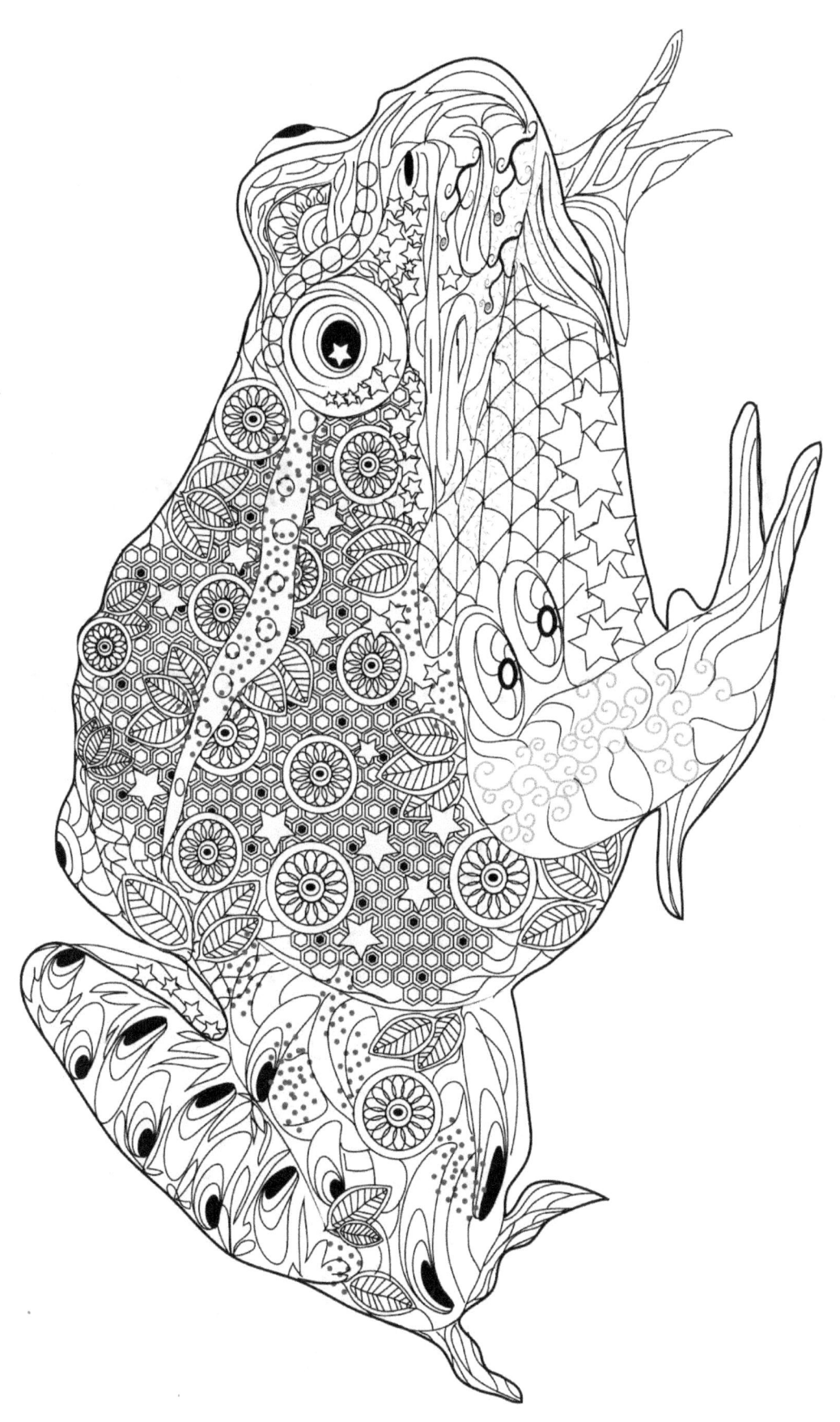

When you stop and look
around this life is pretty
amazing.

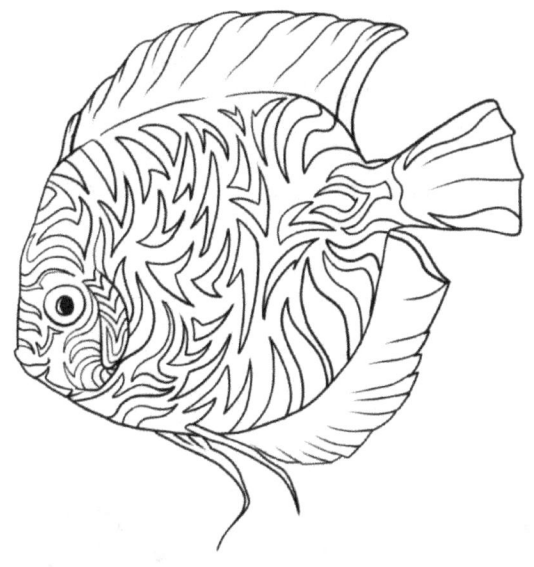

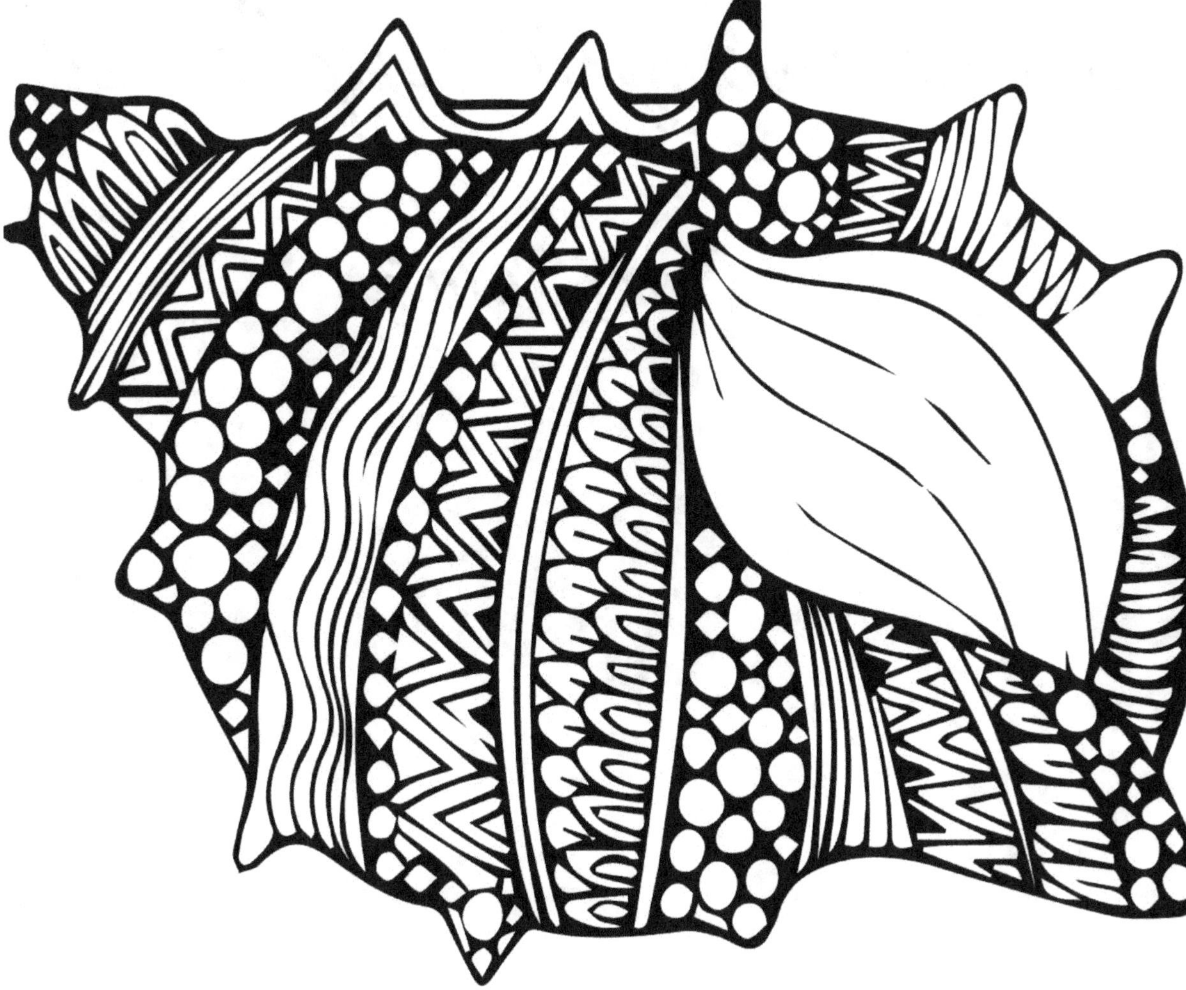

Life is really simple but, we insist on making it complicated.
~ Confucius

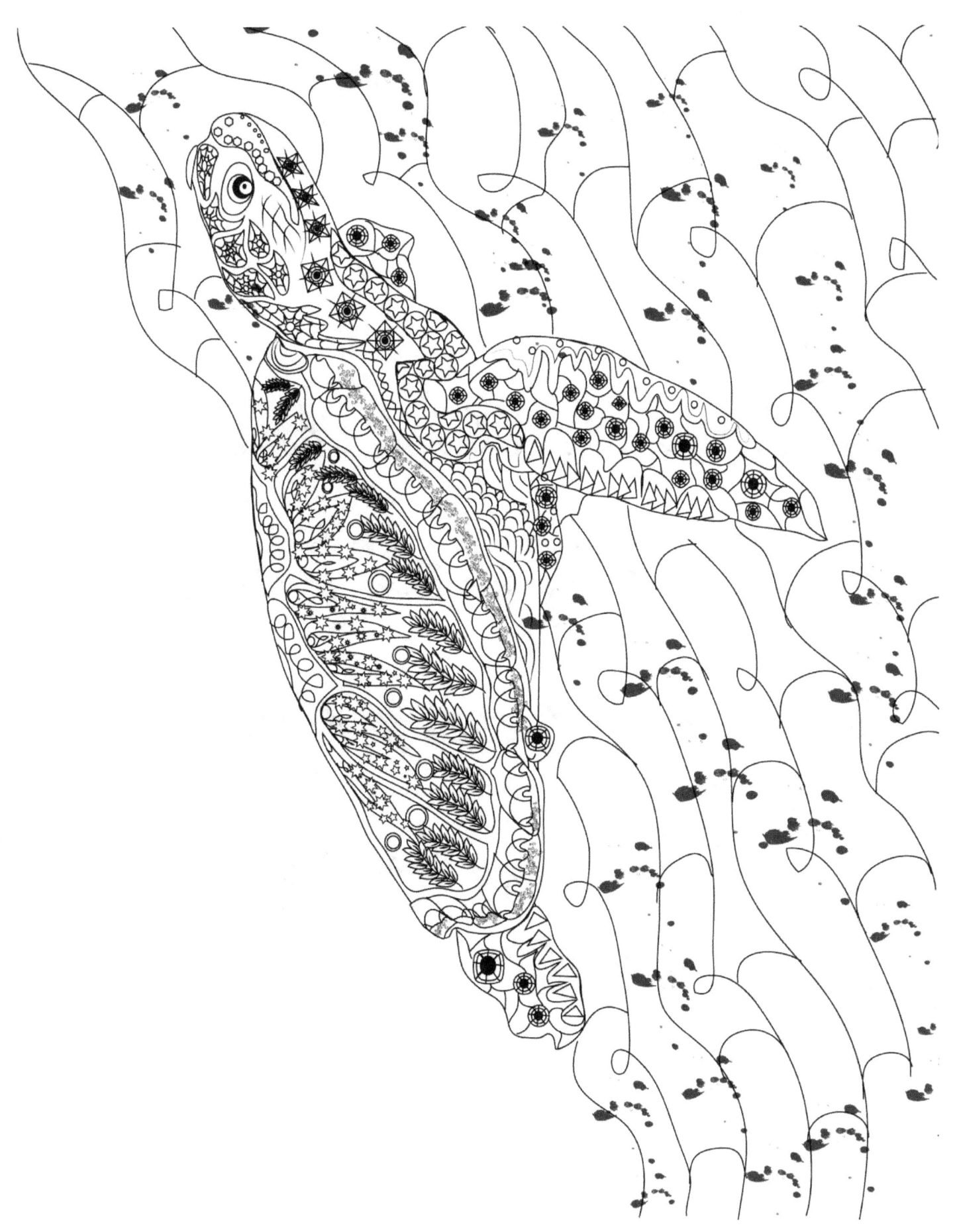

Tell me the story about how the sun loved the moon so much he died every night just to let her breathe.

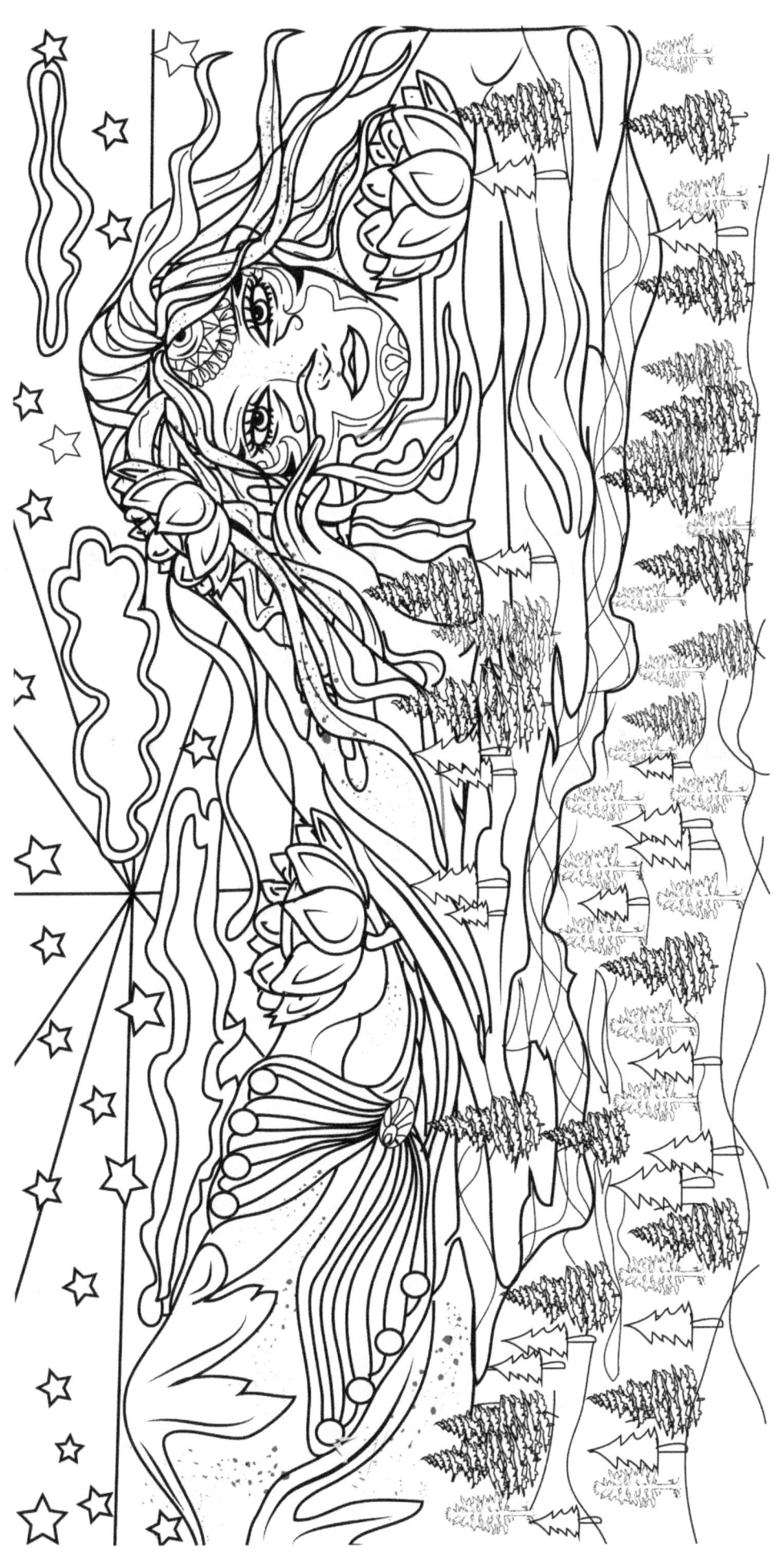

People who hide their feeling

usually care the most.

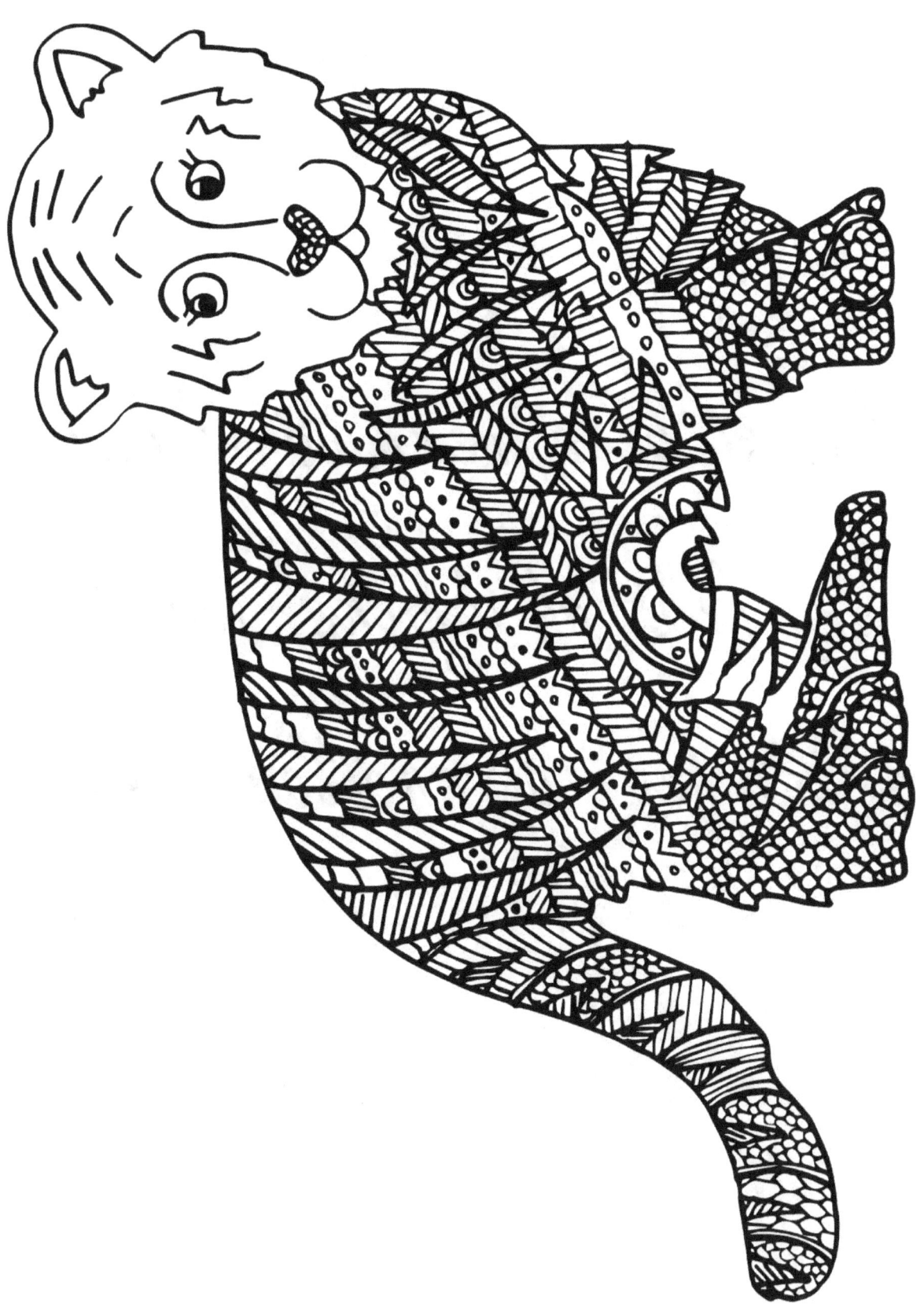

I must be a mermaid; I have no fear of depths, and a great fear of shallow living.

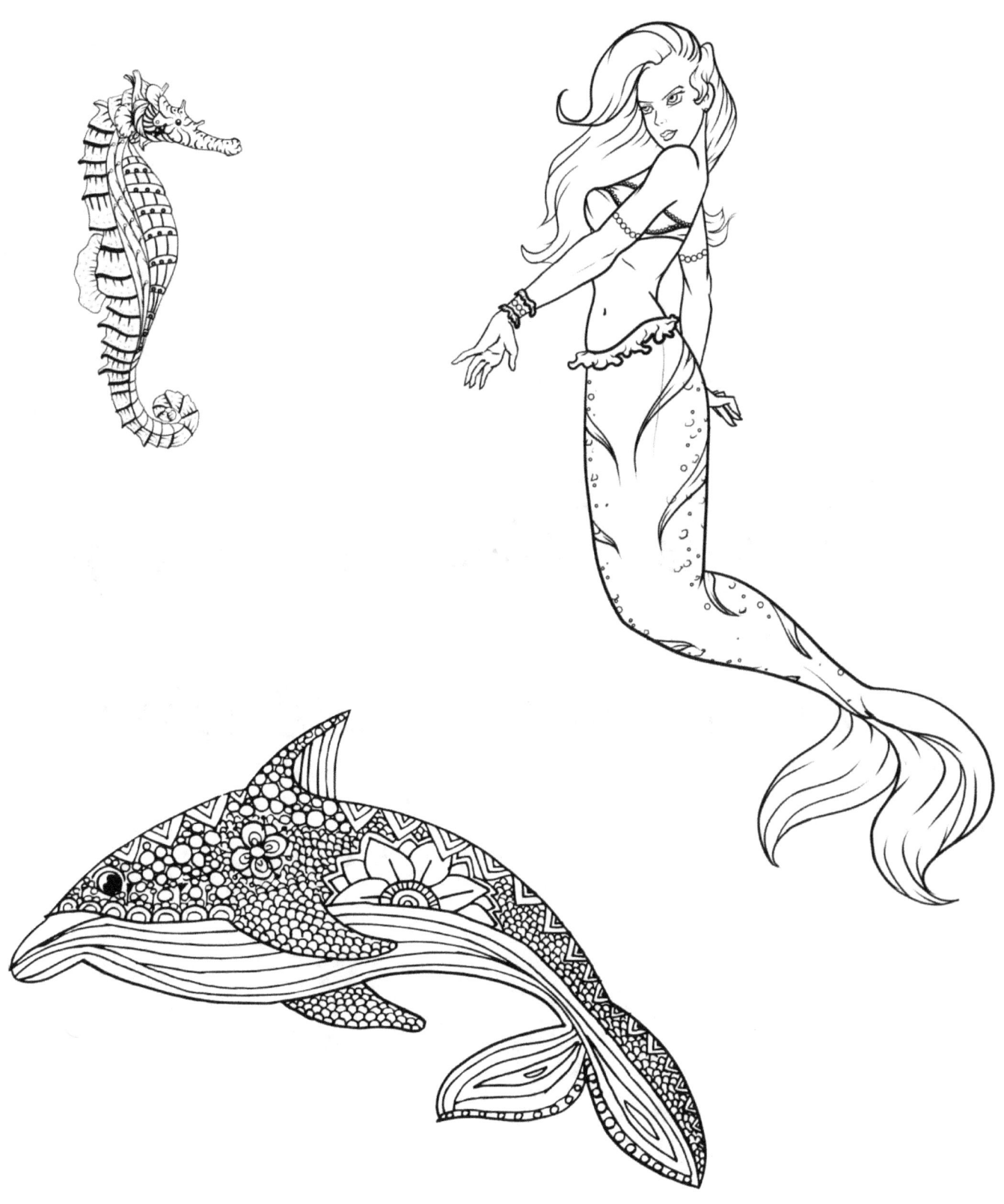

The soul that sees beauty

may sometimes walk alone.

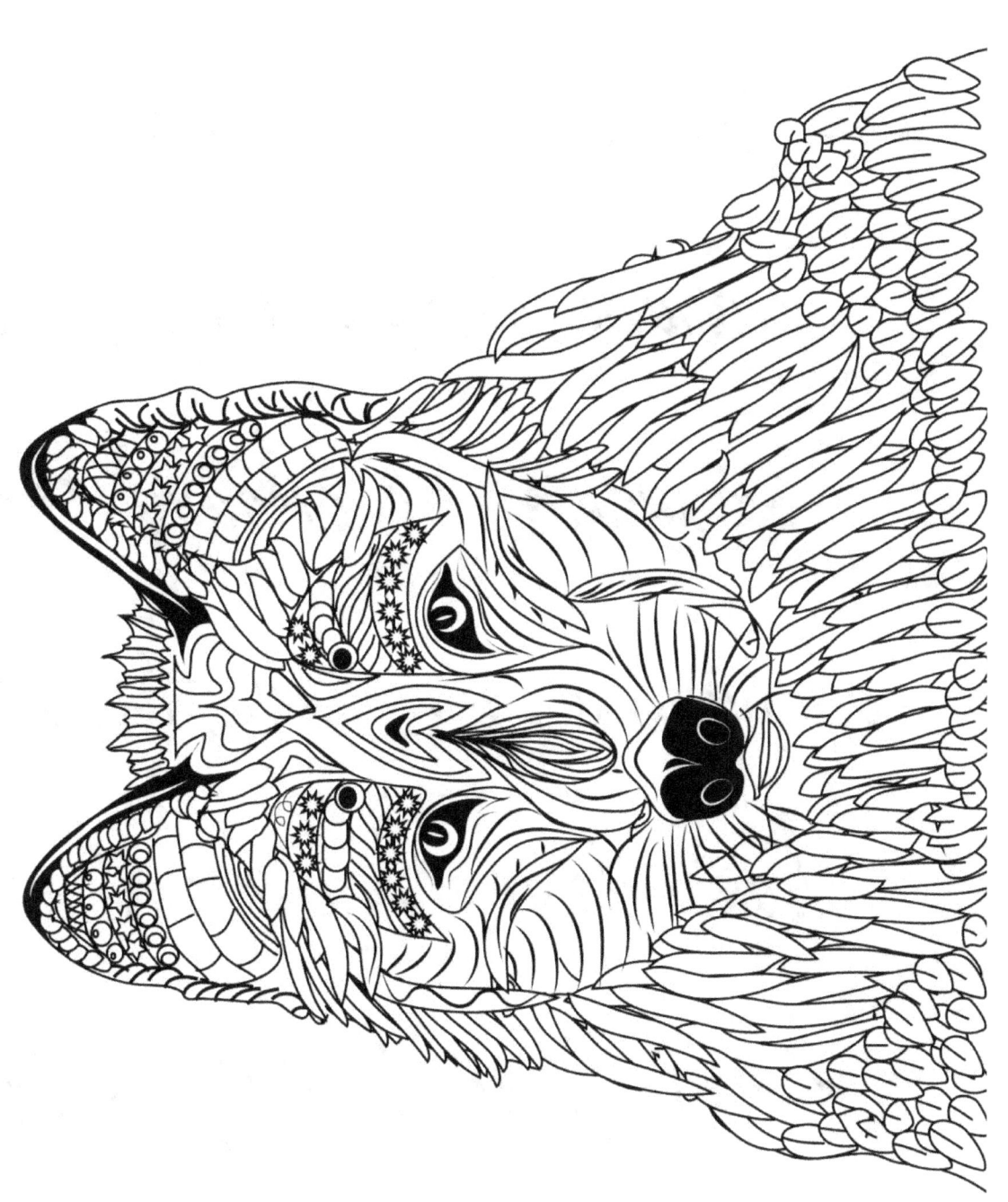

Advice from a river; go with the flow, immerse yourself in nature. Slow down and meander, go around the obstacles. Be thoughtful of those downstream and stay current. The beauty is in the journey.

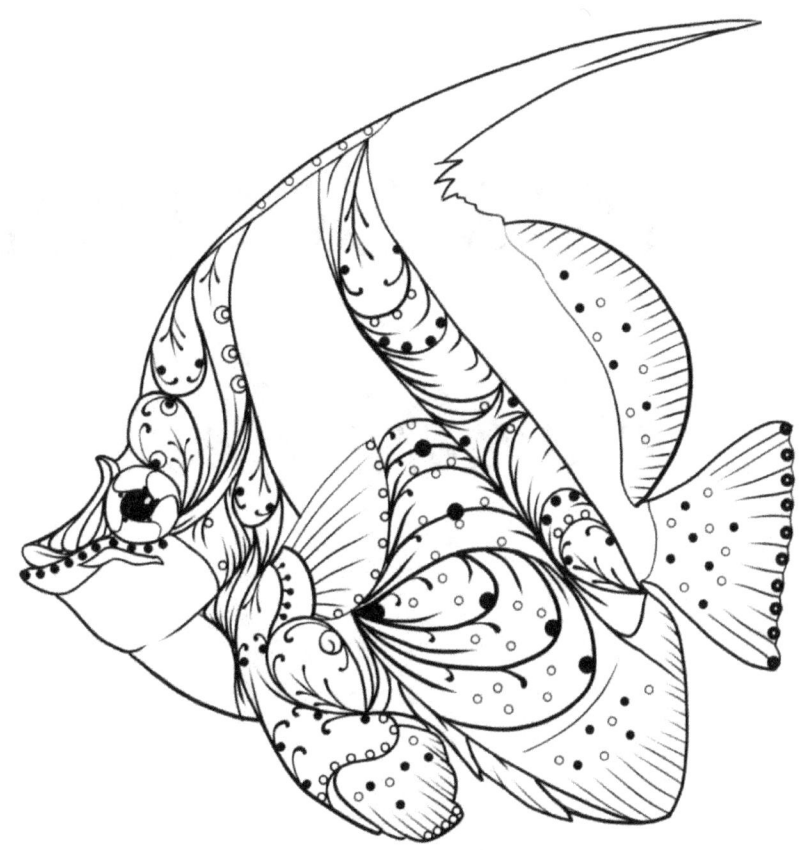

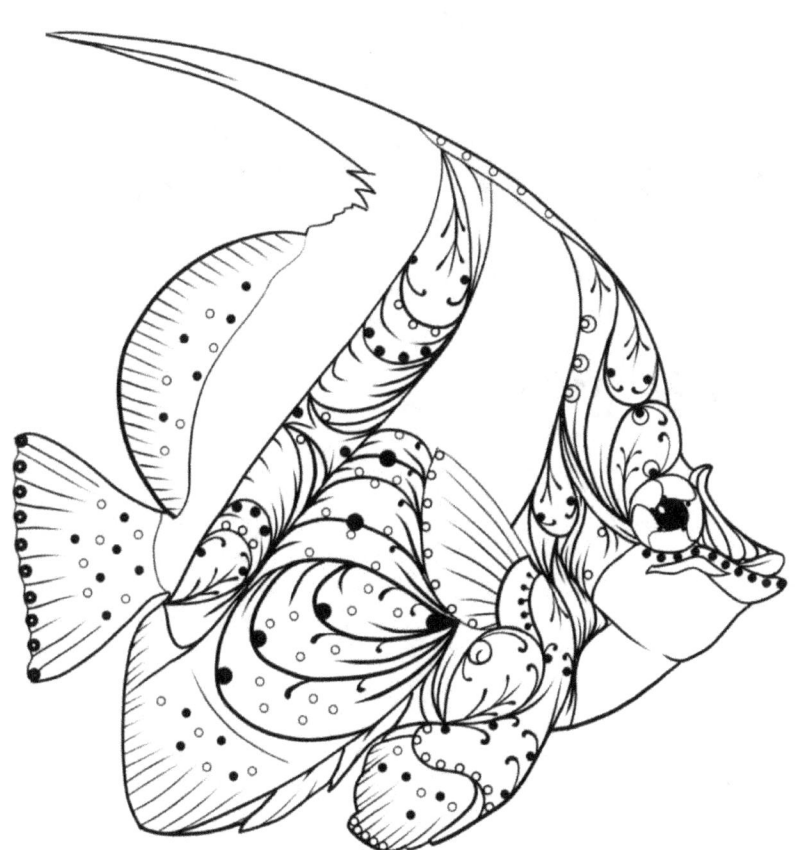

# Bonus Section

## 15 Mandala Designs

Write all of your secrets in the sand and trust them to the sea.

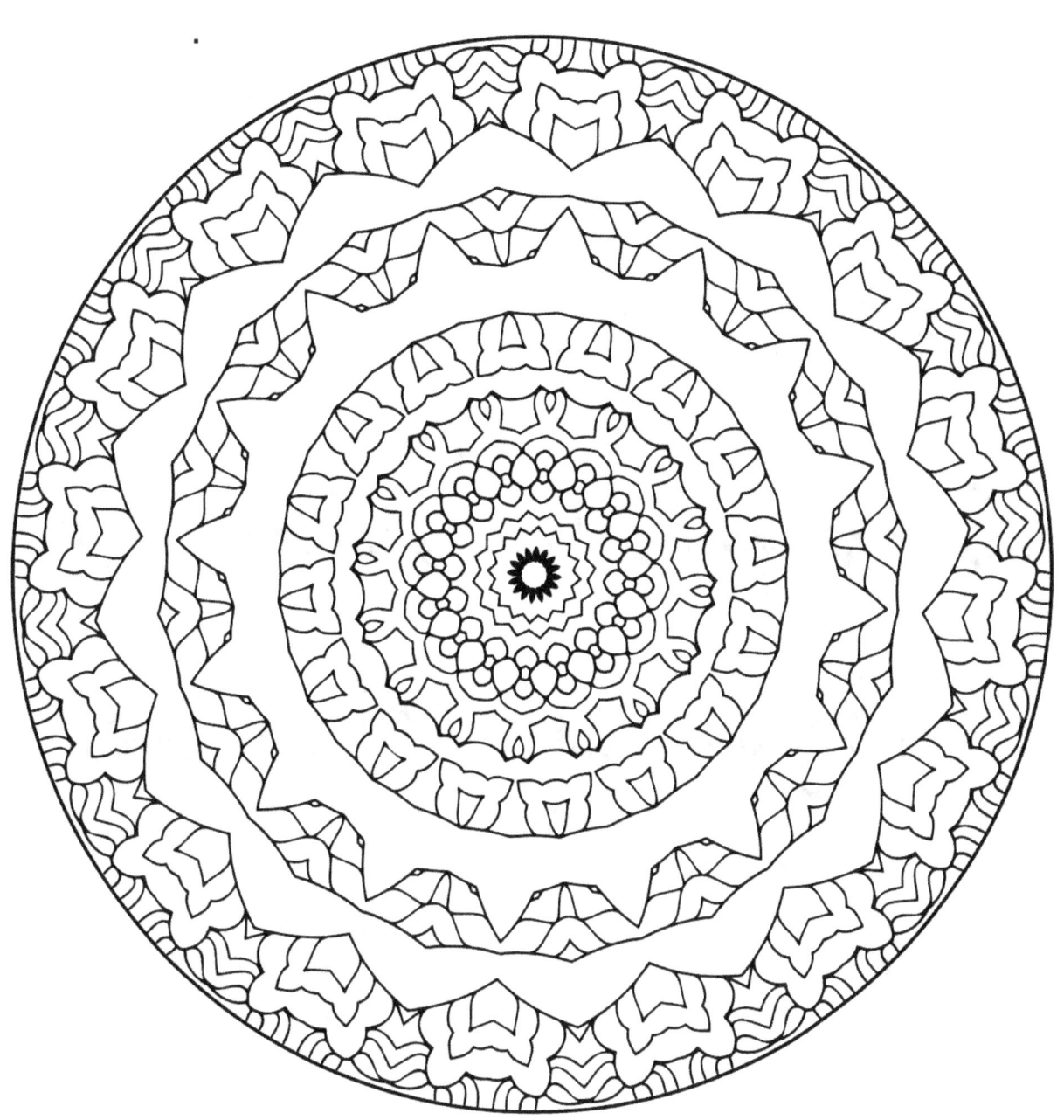

Art is not what you see but, what you make others see.

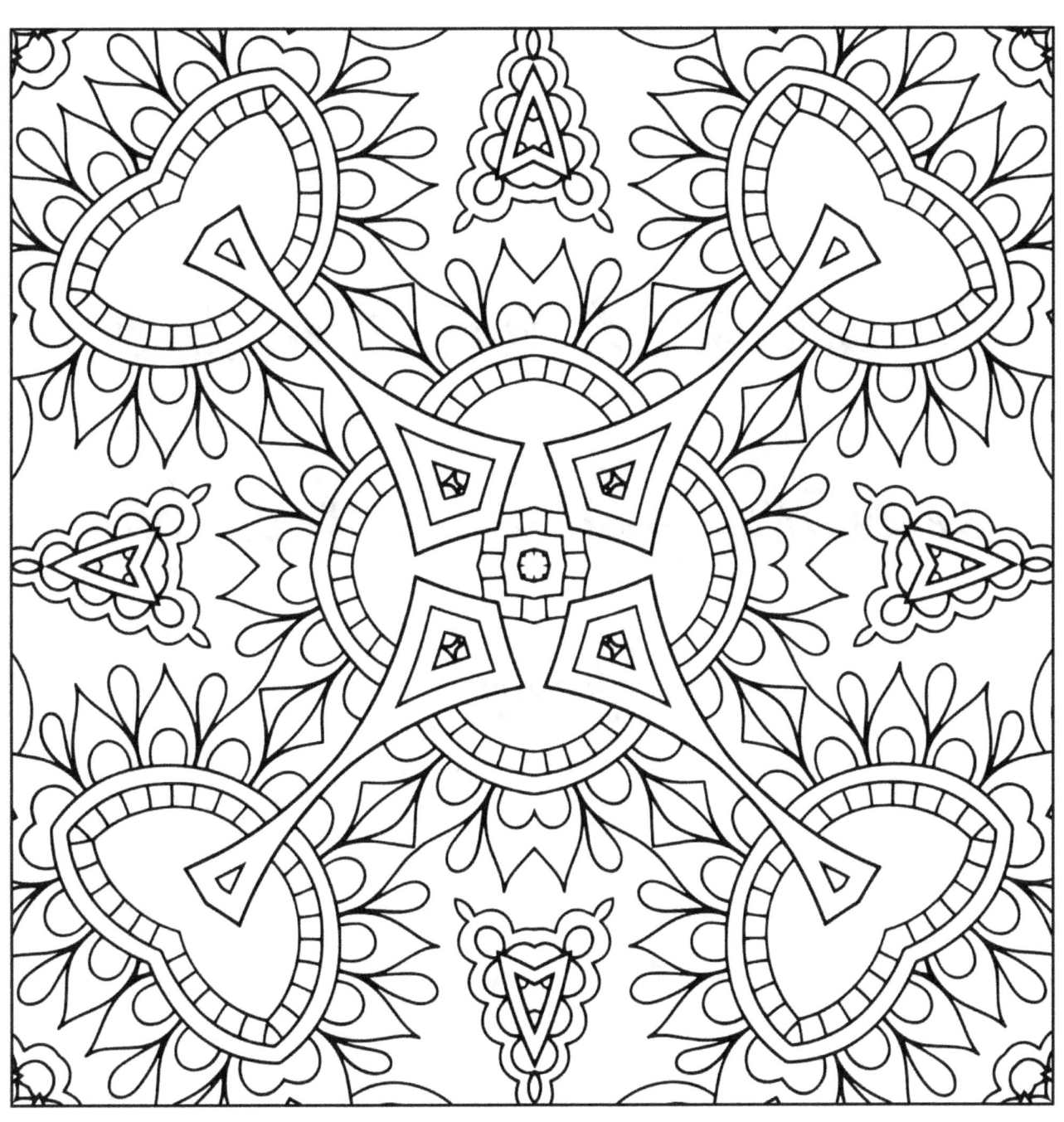

I just need some time in a beautiful place to clear my head.

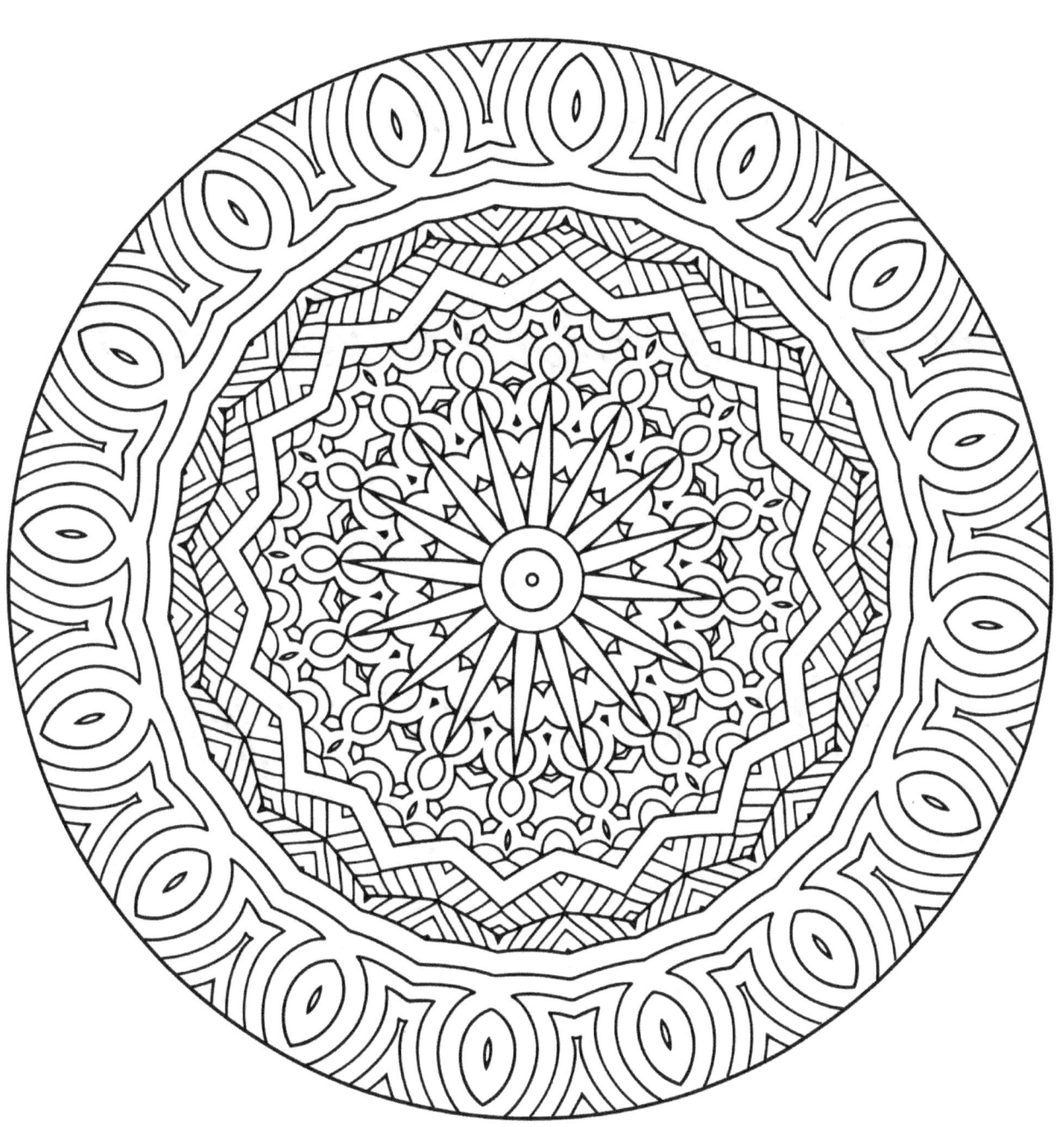

The difficulty lies not so much in developing new ideas as in escaping old ones.
~ John Maynard Keynes

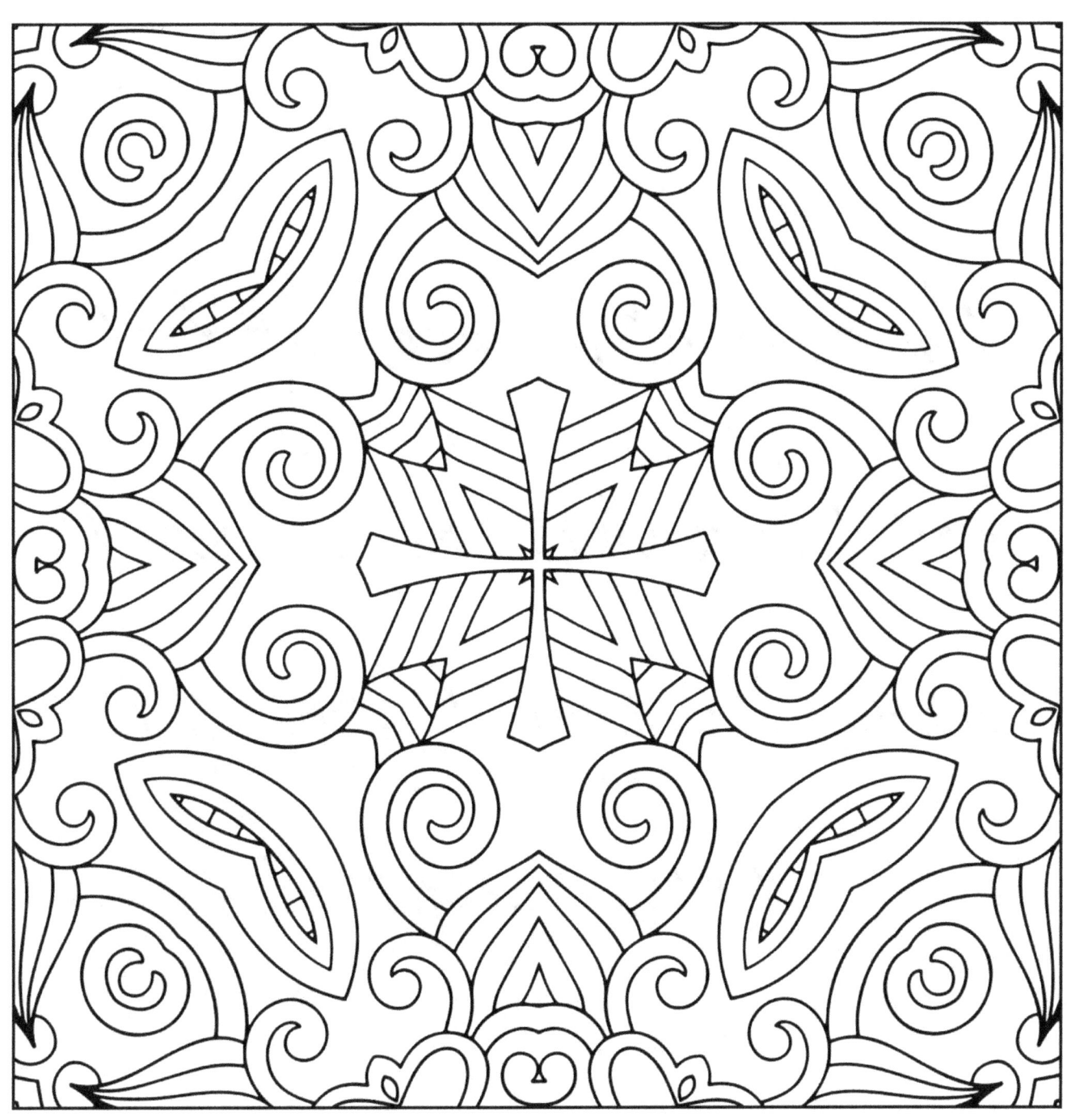

I'm a great believer of luck and I find that the harder I work, the more I have of it.
~ Thomas Jefferson

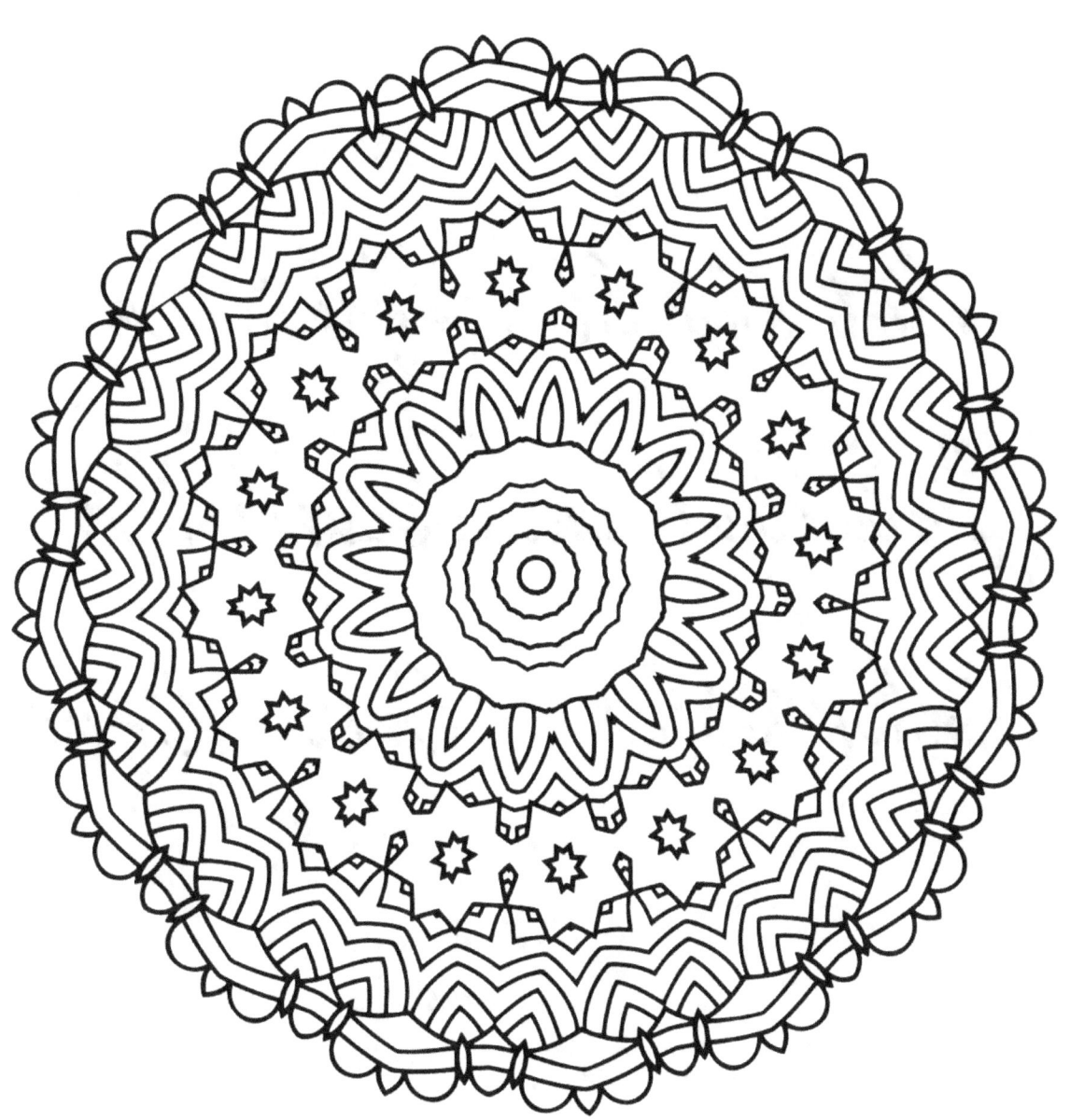

Art should comfort the disturbed and disturb the comfortable. ~ Cesar Cruz

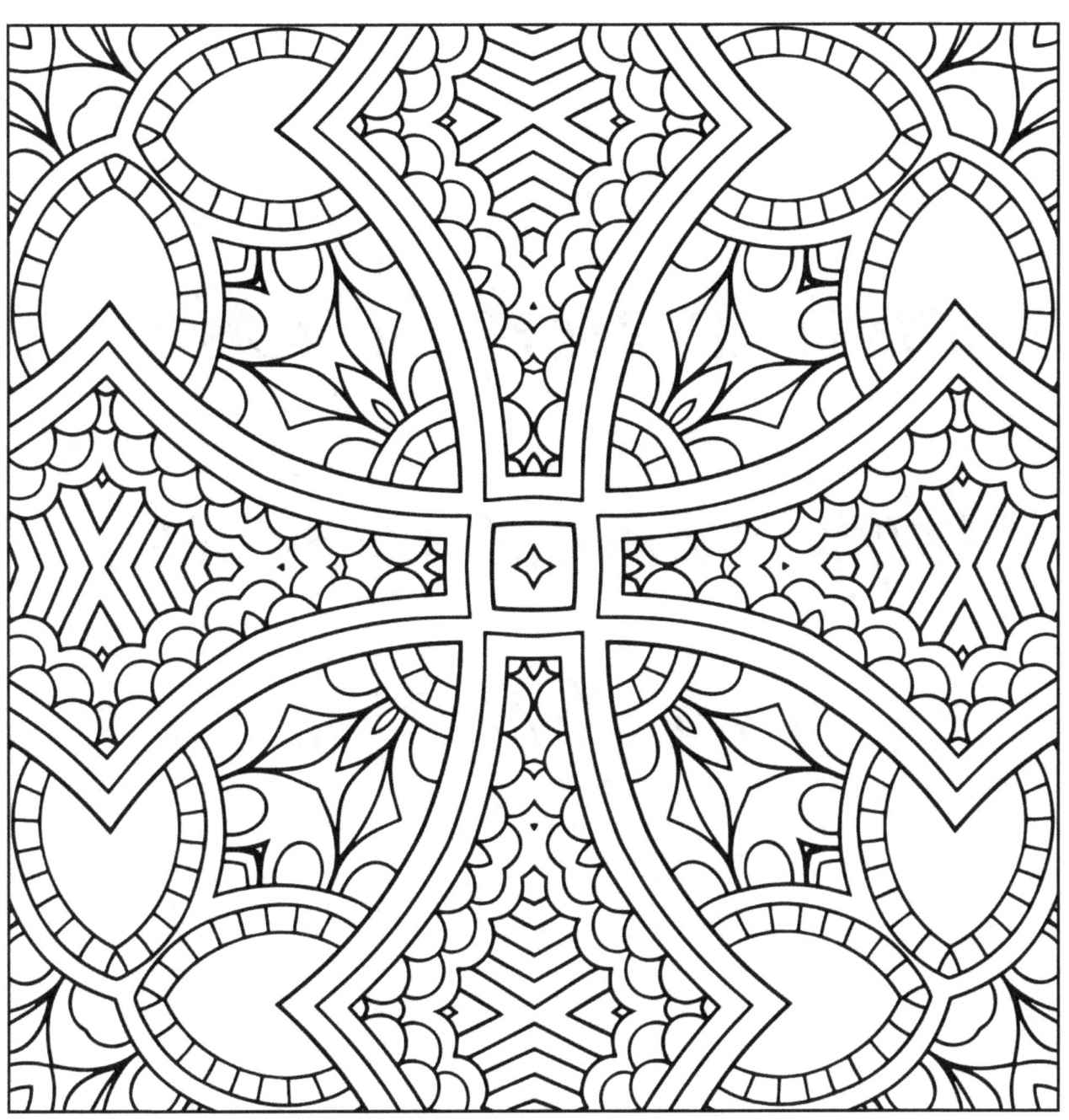

Make at least one person

happy each and every day.

Even if it's you.

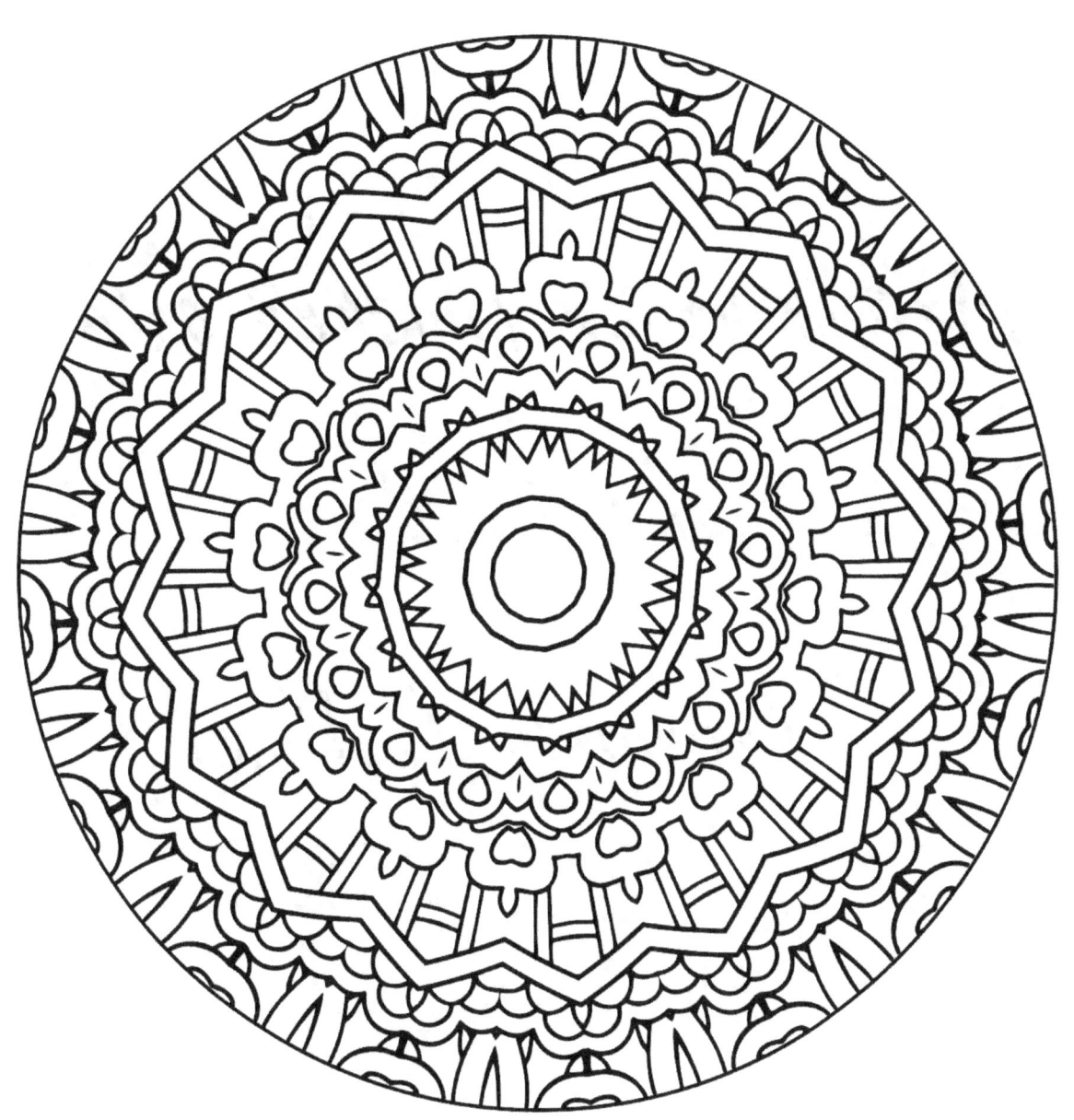

Art is never finished only

abandoned.

~ Leonardo da Vinci

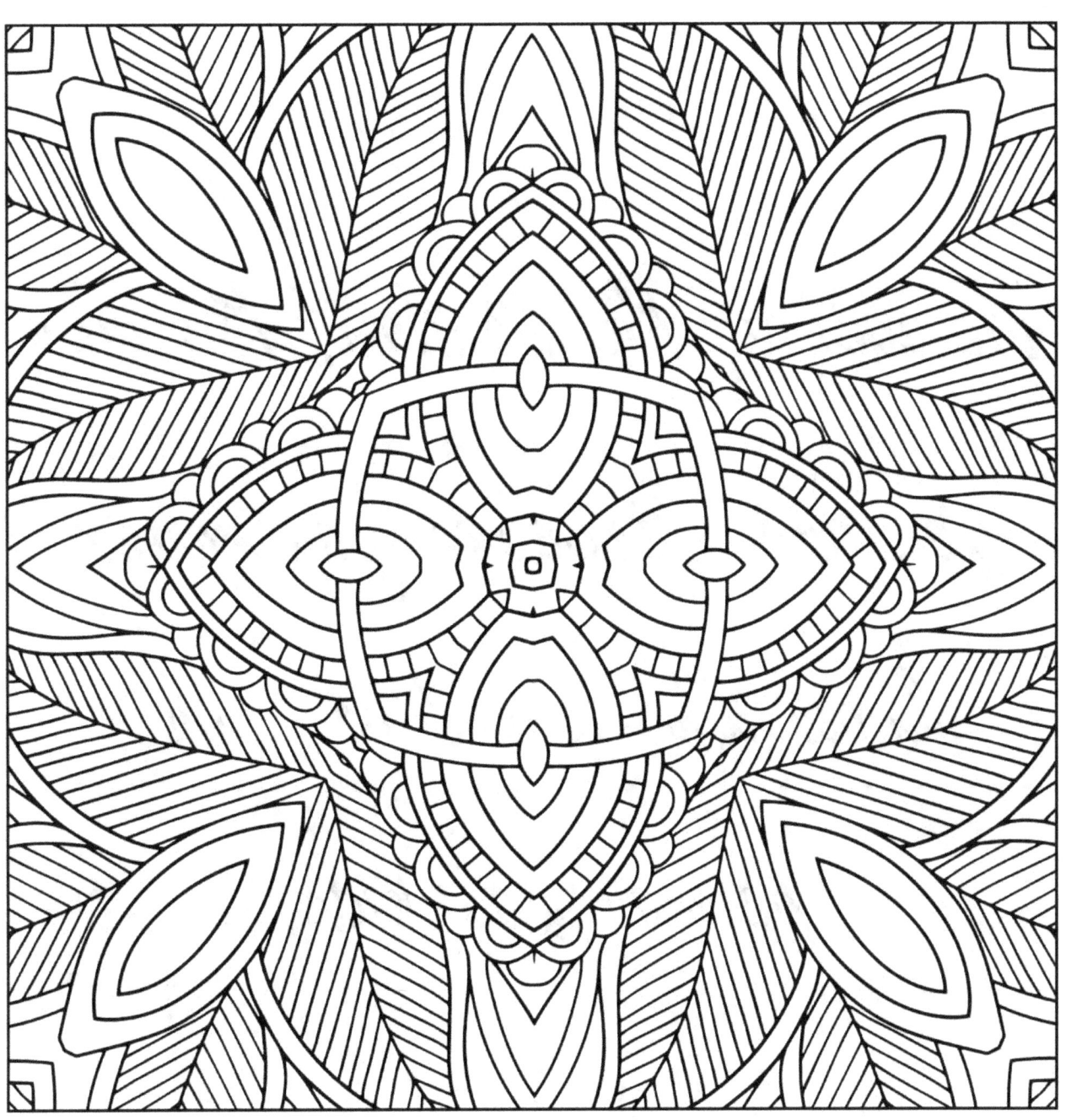

Be weird. Be random. Be who you are. Because you never know who would love the person you hide.

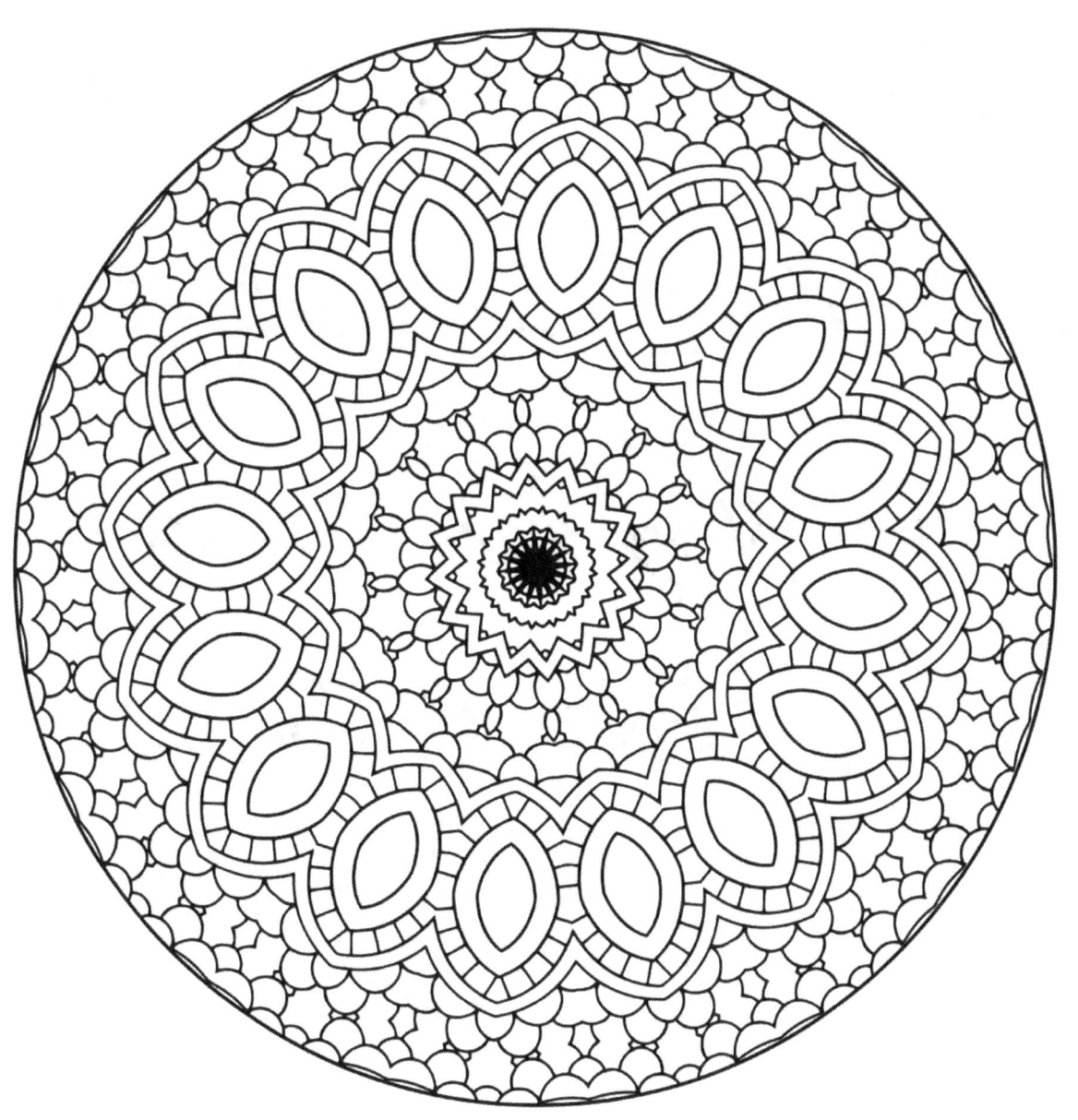

Don't waste your time on
explanations, people only hear
what they want to hear.
~ Paulo Coelbo

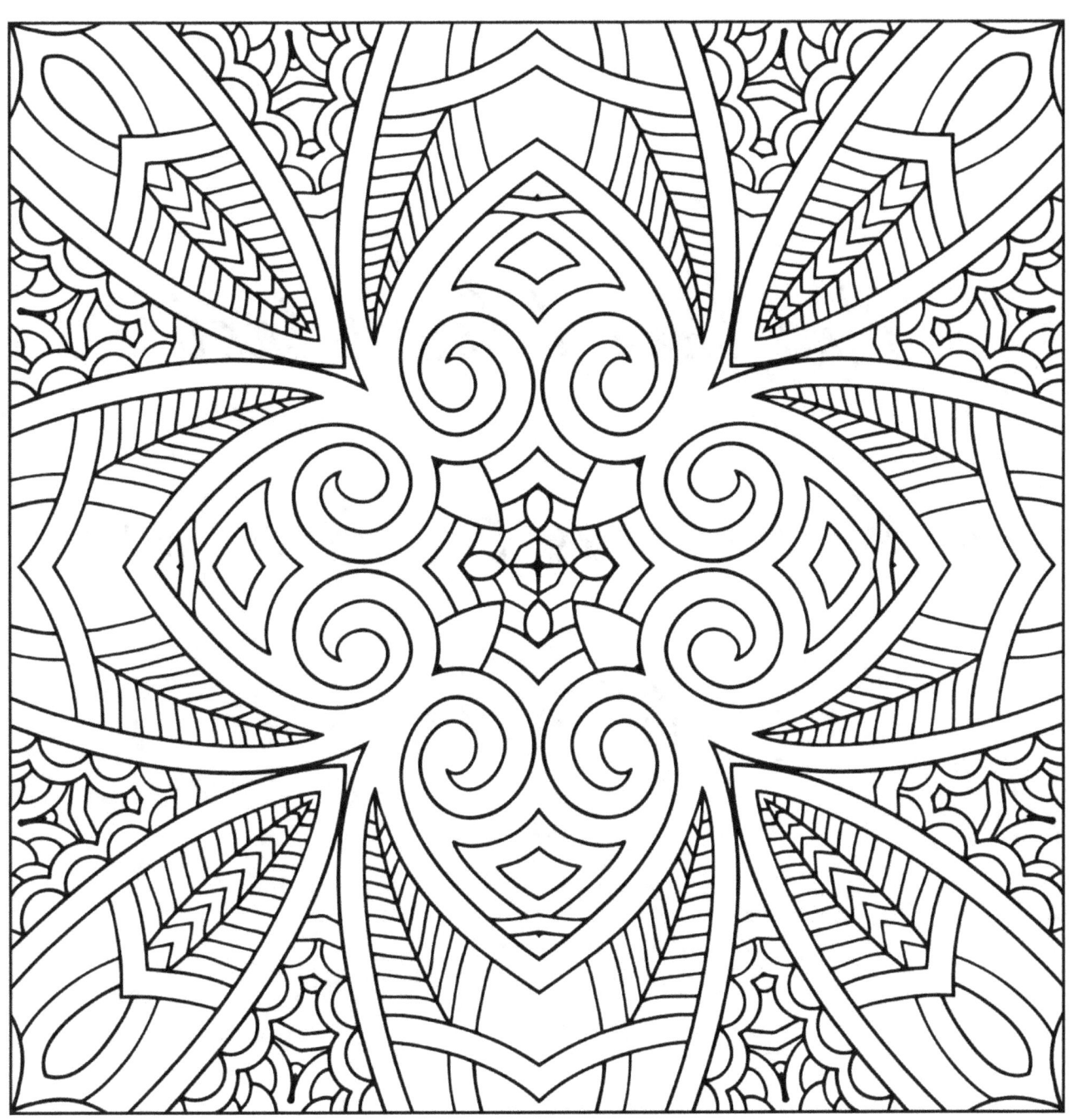

And then I found that

adventure was the best way

to learn.

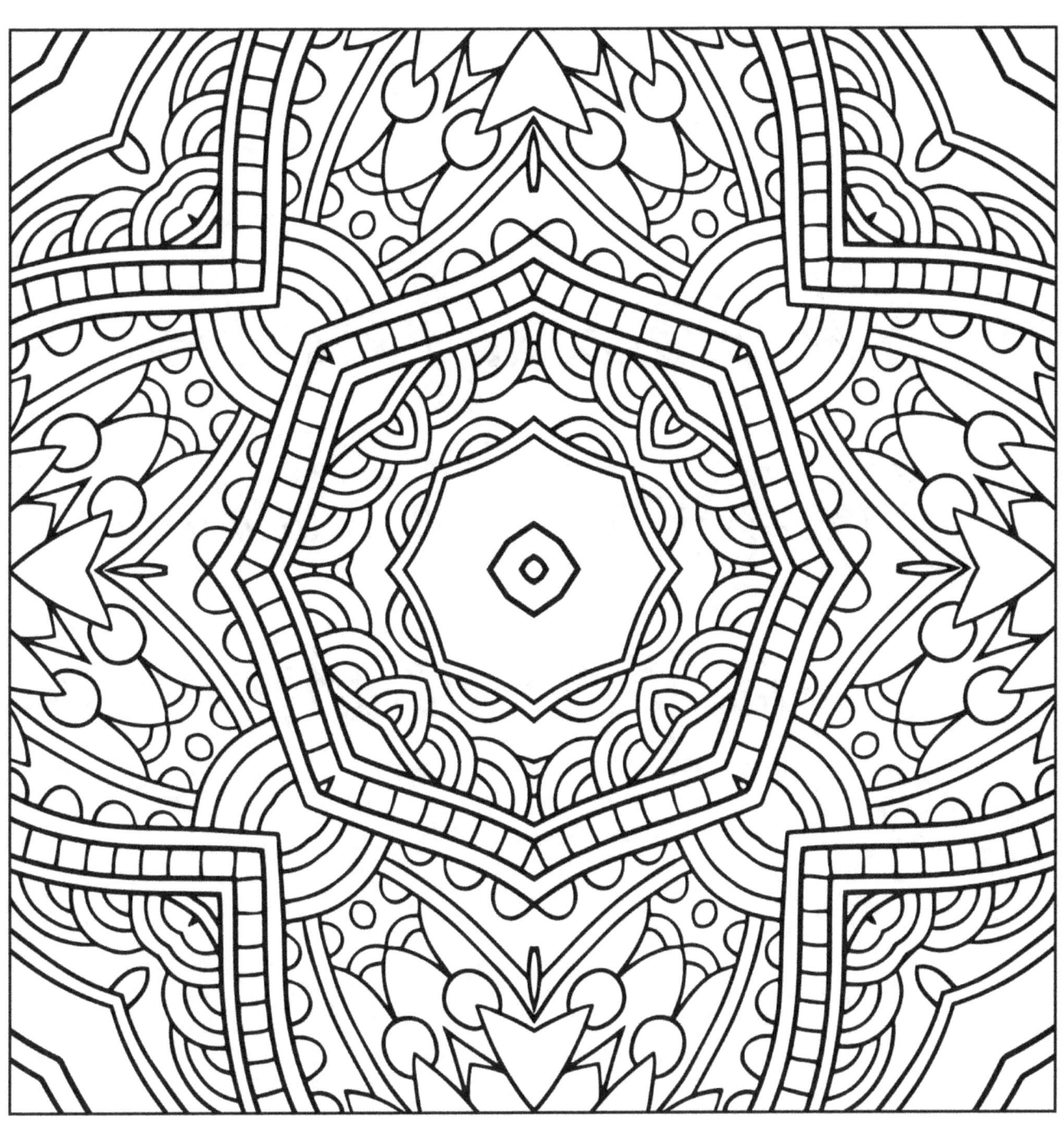

The brave may not live forever, but the cautious don't live at all.

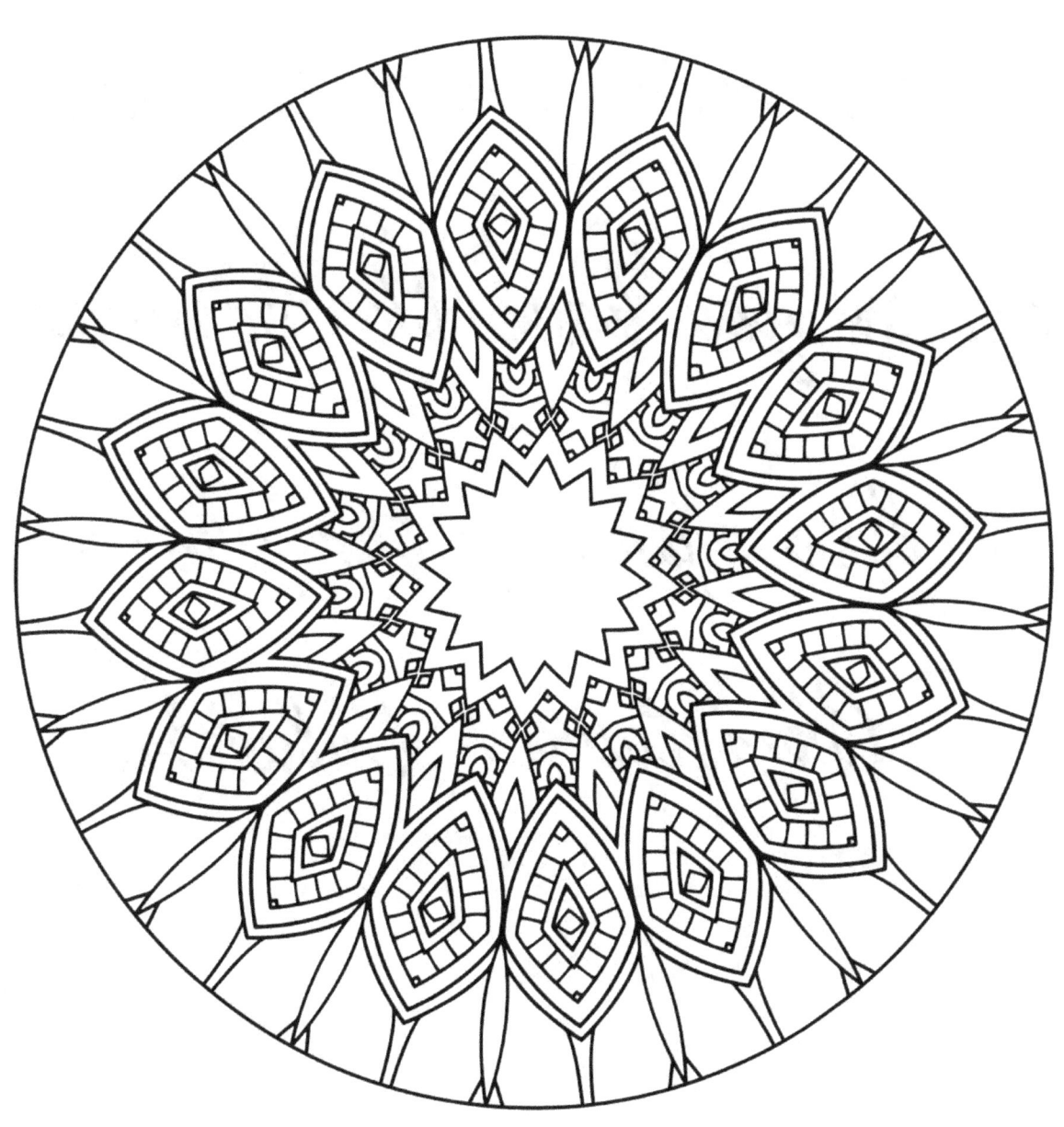

You can never cross the ocean
unless you have the courage
to lose sight of the shore.
~ Christopher Columbus

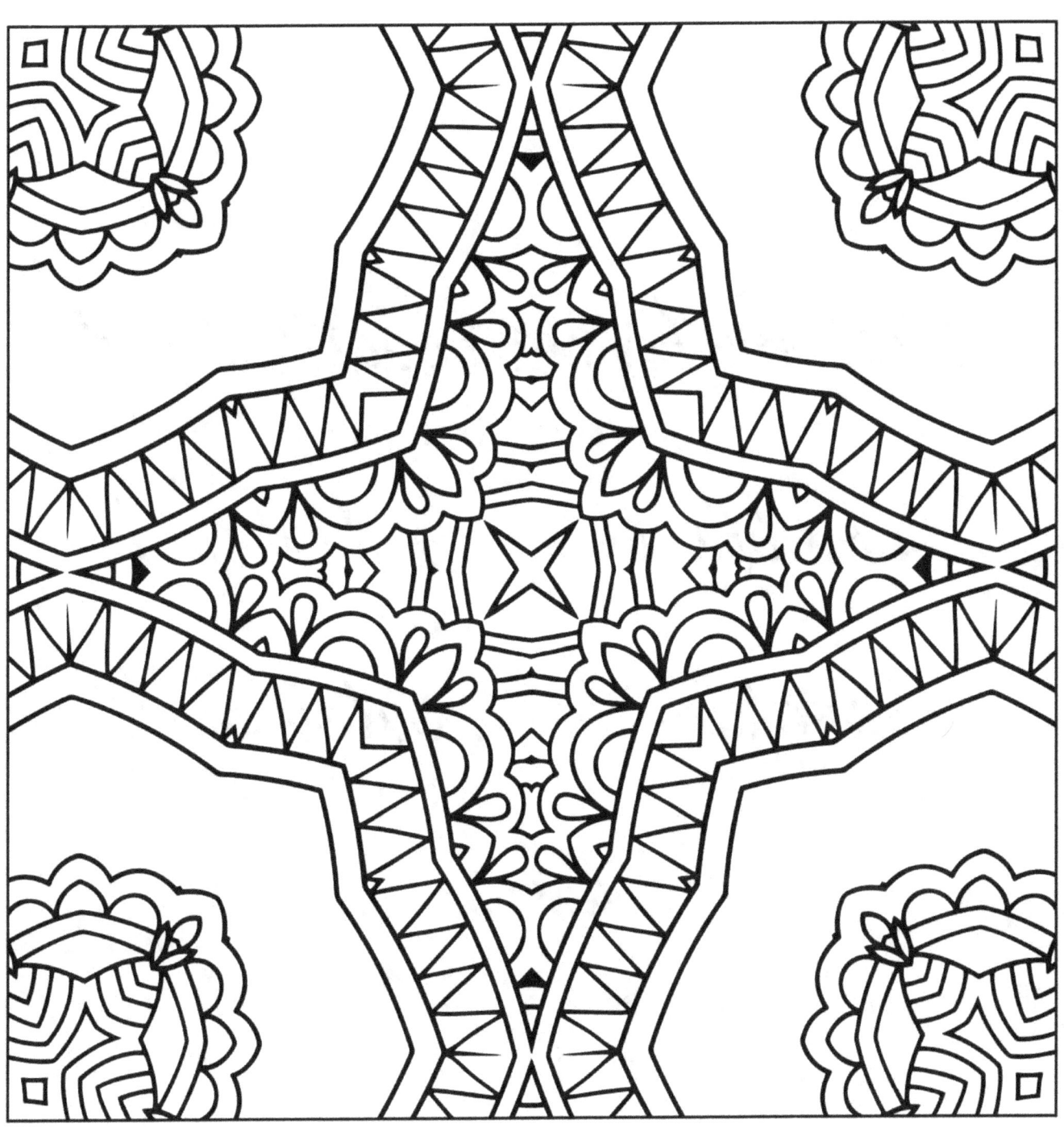

The truth is a beautiful and terrible thing, and should therefore be treated with caution.

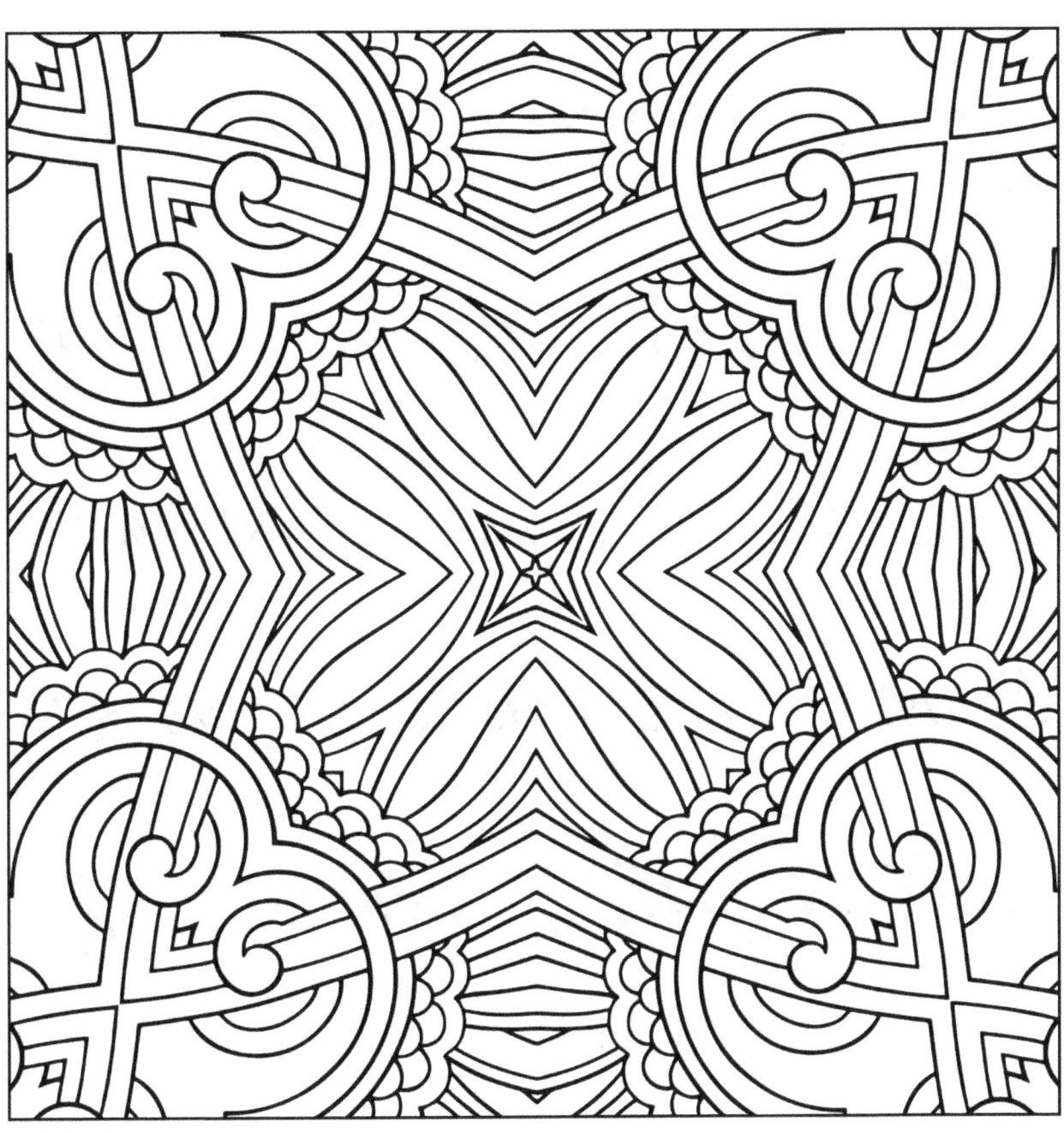

You can close your eyes to the things you do not want to see, but you cannot close your heart to the things you do not want to feel. ~ Johnny Depp

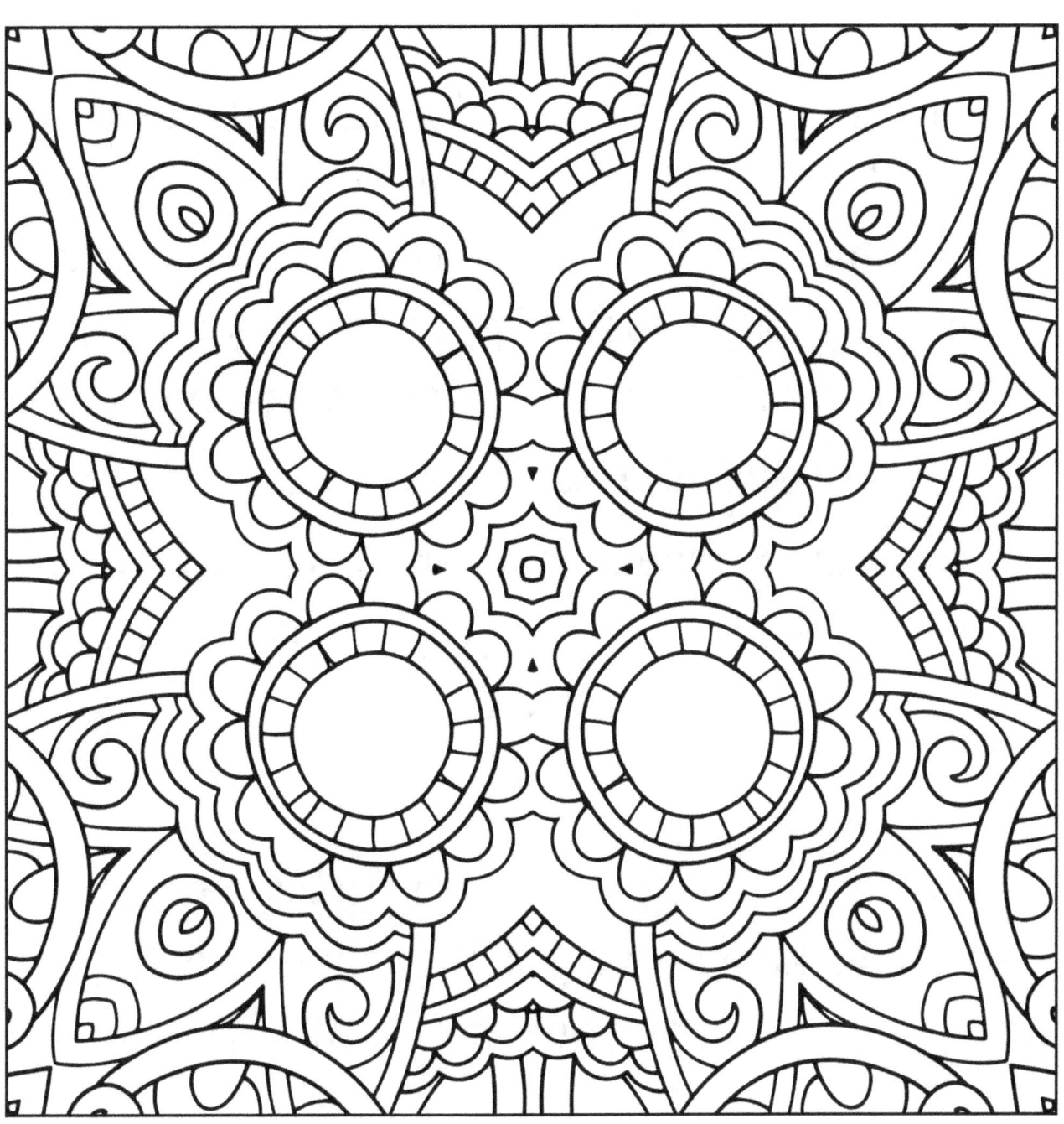

I hope you enjoyed this book just as much as I did creating it. Look for more to come in the series shortly.

Also soon to come: A coloring challenge to have the cover picture on my next book, there will be multiple prizes to be announced shortly (so everybody wins). If you would like to join the contest sign up by sending me an email to lovingtheoutdoors2013@gmail.com

That is my personal email and I would love to get any feed back to help me create the next book.

Also please leave a review on Amazon.com and let others know what you thought of this book. Thank you very much!